Growing Up in
Washington, D.C.

An Oral History

Splashing around Columbus Monument at Union Station Plaza, 1960. (Courtesy Gallagher Collection, HSW Collections.)

Growing Up in Washington, D.C.

An Oral History

The Historical Society of Washington, D.C.

Edited by Jill Connors

With a foreword by

Dolores Kendrick, Poet Laureate of Washington, D.C.

TEMPUS

Published by Arcadia Publishing,
an imprint of Tempus Publishing, Inc.
2 Cumberland Street
Charleston, SC 29401

Printed in Great Britain.

Library of Congress Catalog Card Number: 2001095451

For all general information contact Arcadia Publishing at:
Telephone 843-853-2070
Fax 843-853-0044
E-Mail sales@arcadiapublishing.com

For customer service and orders:
Toll-Free 1-888-313-2665

Visit us on the internet at http://www.arcadiapublishing.com

ON THE COVER (INSET): *Breena and Vicki Clarke cooling off after a long summer day, 1958. (Courtesy of Breena Clarke.)*

ON THE COVER (BACKGROUND): *Enjoying a visit to the Tidal Basin and the view of the Jefferson Memorial, c. 1940. (Courtesy of Zack Spratt Collection, HSW Collections.)*

CONTENTS

FOREWORD

PIECES OF THE PAST

There were the solemn streets of LeDroit Park sweetened by well-kept houses, homes of genteel folk who were yet to be called "Black" or "African-American," who defined themselves as "Colored" and were proud of it. Their rituals of community embraced high education, respect for elders, baseball (until noon) on weekends in the courtyard hugged on the edges of the flat, grass-struggling yard by the neighborhood houses. (That meant the back parts of the three-hundred block of U, Fourth, and T Streets.) Here the extended family of semi-professionals and career educators whose mere presence patterned a calling to the young folk to "make something of yourself" did justice to our heritage and hope.

There were the U Street Evenings and the Snowball Man pushing his cart through the streets as it carried a block of ice to be shaved to a min-taste and covered with syrupy green or orange or red or yellow stuff, or all four, that cooled our heated bodies in the Washington summer and the time of no air conditioning. The snowball was worth the nickel. Then the Watermelon Man, strolling his rickety machine while singing his seductive aria to the sweating families of the neighborhood: Sweet Watermelon,/Come taste mine,/Sweeter than honey/And just off the vine! At mid-week and on weekends came baseball at Griffith Stadium. It was then that my brother Bobby began his life as a young entrepreneur, for he sold shelled peanuts with my Uncle Jack, who held the concession. After the game he would go through the stands and pick up the shelled peanuts dropped by the fans, reselling them at the next game.

In the 400 block of U Street were a block of lawned, detached houses resembling small manors. In one of them lived Garnett C. Wilkerson, school superintendent of the second district, the public school district for Colored. (The first District was assigned to Whites.) Under his administration and that of those who preceded and followed him emerged Dunbar High, college prep and called the Phillips Exeter of public schools; Armstrong High, for students interested in the manual arts and from which Duke Ellington graduated; and for those students interested in a business career, Cardozo High. These were the Great Three, efficient, well-run schools, staffed by highly committed Black teachers, with students who were highly motivated although they were products of a segregated school system that ironically cast them into the distinction of being the best educational institutions in the city.

All of this, of course, led in one direction: The Hill. Perched at the top of Fourth to Seventh Streets like a Black Acropolis were Howard University and Miner Teachers College, where there the Negro sages walked in a quiet splendor, all of whom had broken the racist barriers in the ivy league colleges and universities and returned to Washington to educate their own. I was one of them (both at Dunbar and Miner), enveloped in the unrelenting energy of those times of Sterling Brown, the great poet and teacher; Euphemia L. Haynes, the first Black woman to graduate from Smith College; Frank Snowden, the renown classics scholar; Alain Locke, philosopher and writer; Charles Drew, who developed blood plasma; Emmett Everett Just, scientist and marine biologist, and the only person in his time to graduate magna cum laude from Dartmouth (and whose image is now on a U.S. postage stamp). Except for Dr. Haynes and Sterling Brown (who was my father's tennis partner) I had not met or studied under any of these scholars, nor had I met Paul Lawrence Dunbar, the poet, who early in his career spent some of this time in the home of Kelly Miller, a dean of the university. But now, as I recall these times, I know that my family and I were at the center of a kind of Washington Renaissance, comparable in its way to that which was already evolving in Harlem. Mary McLeod Bethune had come to Washington and urged students at a Dunbar assembly to take their professionalism and talents seriously and to refuse to give in to anything that would weaken self-esteem. It was as though, at that moment, these passionate energies had arrived at a time when a magnetic attraction roamed the genius of these sages to bleed into that generation of young Black men and women whose buoyant destiny in the city of Washington was about to be called. And I was one of them following the established paths, often scratching out my own to the delight of my parents and the watchful eye of the neighborhood.

THE CITY WITH TWO FACES

The Lichtman Theatres on the other U Street supplied films for the community, since Blacks were not allowed to attend the movies in downtown, white movie houses. But we had the Lincoln, Republic, and Booker T, which showed all the first-rate films usually running them for a week at a time. For 25¢ you could see a film to your heart's content (buckin' the show, we called it). At Sixth and T was the Howard Theatre, a feast of film and live entertainment. Since my uncle managed the Howard, my brother, sister, and I could get in free. I delighted in the big stage shows where the Big Bands thrilled audiences with jazz and swing, where I could hear, third row center, horns gasping, drums speaking, dancers swinging, and Ella and Duke, Count Basie, Nat King Cole, and the colors, the lights crashing onto the brass horns, the spotlights that could make a performer vanish into darkness at the sound of a final poignant note of a song! It was all there, the other U Street where the flesh of entertainment lived and where white people came to integrate without noticing the incongruity of that journey, without a whimper, especially in those moments when their own entertainment failed them. "Café Society Uptown" my father (who was known as dean of Washington's Negro Press) wrote in his newspaper, the *Gailey News*, later to become the *Spotlight*, which along with the *Afro-American* (now in its 52nd year) chronicled the times of the Black cultural community.

There it was, all in my little sense of prosperity that for me meant that life was secure and predictable under the skin of my adolescent dreams and determination.

THE FINAL NEIGHBORHOODS

So I went. So I ventured. And often I found or discovered the city moving in and around me like the November breezes it uttered to anyone who would listen, or know its darkness and light, in the pit of its misgivings and solemn promises, and undeniable endurance. Yet, I did not know that these neighborhoods were final, shifting even as I spent my energies within their grasp.

There was Foggy Bottom, Georgetown, the contented home of Washington Blacks off the mainstream of Pennsylvania Avenue, Northwest, and the trolley cars and buses that took them downtown. Some of my school friends lived there and we often walked from St. Augustine's Catholic school (an elementary and middle school run by the Oblate Sisters of Providence, the only order of Black nuns in the country at that time) at Fifteenth and S Streets, Northwest through Lafayette Park to Twenty-fifth Street to study together in the quiet living rooms of the elders. Our appointments were clearly our own, so we were free, for instance, to enjoy a summer National Symphony concert from the Memorial Bridge overlooking what was then called Watergate. Since we couldn't afford tickets, we would rent bikes and cycle to the bridge to listen to the orchestra that performed from a barge. Other evenings my mother would take brother, my sister, and me to a garden party at the now historical Metropolitan Baptist Church on R Street, Northwest. Because my paternal grandmother was a church member and she always paid her church dues, we could get delicious summers suppers without charge and linger amongst the grown-ups, the lawn tables, hanging lanterns, and lightening bugs.

Some of my friends lived in the old Washington Southwest, a thriving, solemn middle-class community, known for its conservative homes and liberal black residents. Then there were Seventeenth and Eighteenth Streets, Northwest, where from P to Massachusetts to Dupont Circle the great mansions peered down upon me wherever I walked from my maternal grandmother's apartment on S and Eighteenth to Fifteenth and M to St. Augustine's for Mass. My cousins and I thought there were ghosts in those mansions, particularly on dark winter mornings, and we scurried past them as though there were dragons with tongues of fire and apparitions. On Seventeenth Street, intersected at R and S, were the residences of old, established Black families, and Corcoran Street, stretching from Fourteenth to Sixteenth, was a neighborhood of working-class Blacks who imposed an ownership that was suspicious of strangers.

The times that Blacks ventured out of these neighborhoods to go downtown were to shop at Hecht's, Kann's, and Lansburgh's, none of which would allow them to eat at their stand-up eating bars, except at a segregated section at the very end. To buffer this my mother usually gave us lunch before we left home, as under no circumstances would she allow our dignity to be abused, for she and my family considered racism to be an obscenity, and we were never allowed to entertain obscenities in any shape or form.

CITY IN A STATE OF GRACE

These were the times: Josephine, my mother, teaching music at St. Augustine's during the summer session, and later writing with Al Fisher and Shep Allen the song, *My Heart Beats for You*, which launched Billy Eckstein's career at the Howard Theatre; my father playing tennis with Sterling Brown at Banneker Tennis Court, the only court open to Blacks; my brother in his budding independence at Griffith Stadium; my sister Juanita, estranged from all this but inching her way toward what she was later to become, the family great. As for the city, it was magnificent, was gentle, was beautiful, was harsh, was simultaneously in poverty and wealth, discrimination and acceptance, was reaching toward its self-orientation and cleansing as it struggled, in the words of poet Gwendolyn Brooks, "Having first to civilize a space/in which to play your violin with grace."

—Dolores Kendrick
Poet Laureate of Washington, D.C.

Howard University at the center of Washington's Renaissance. (Courtesy HSW Collections, CHS 4733.)

9

ACKNOWLEDGMENTS

This book grew out of a series of projects, including a community oral history initiative and an exhibition. Adrienne DeArmas envisioned an oral history project focused on childhood in Washington to celebrate the 200th anniversary of the city becoming the national capital, the turning of the millennium, and plans to create the City Museum of Washington, D.C. The City Museum, opening in 2003 in the historic Carnegie Library at Mount Vernon Square, is a new way for the Historical Society of Washington to serve its community by giving the city an accessible and relevant past. It will continue the work of the Historical Society with exhibits, a research library, and educational programs but will move beyond the traditional historical museum role by creating neighborhood gateways with local institutions and partnering with area organizations to extend the museum into the community. *Growing Up in Washington* based on more than 50 interviews was a wonderful prototype for this new relationship with the community.

Whether growing up in an alley dwelling or an apartment house—there are some universal childhood experiences. The experiences of belonging, celebrating, connecting, learning, playing, and working became the organizing principles for the interviews, as well as the book. Volunteers and interns Brian Joyner, Lynda Lantz, and Danette Sokacich conducted interviews that generated a rare balance of people from different races, ethnicities, neighborhoods, and generations. Washingtonians were thrilled to talk about growing up in the capital city; they had never been asked to share their experiences before.

We wish to thank everyone who supported and participated in the *Growing Up in Washington* oral history project. Without the cooperation of all who shared their experiences and supported this book in each stage of its evolution, the project would have never come to fruition. Adrienne DeArmas envisioned the oral history project, created the organizing themes, and guided the project through its first year. Several interns and volunteers worked closely with Adrienne DeArmas over the course of a year to make the project a success. Jessica Nemeths and Sheila Wickouski spent countless hours doing photo research and editing exhibit text. Jane Levey and Anne Rollins published several of the interviews in the *Washington History* magazine in the fall of 2000. Their hard work and careful editing aided us in the process of creating this book. The incredible staff of HSW deserves more praise than this acknowledgment could possibly offer. They complete heroic tasks on a daily basis, making HSW thrive.

INTRODUCTION

When most Americans think about children in Washington they picture school trips and tour buses at the Smithsonian. But some children never visited Washington, they already lived here. For them, the nation's shrines served as playgrounds. Their memories combine the ordinary pleasures and pains of childhood with the awareness of growing up in a very special place. Washington is a city of people with a rich and multi-layered history. Despite the myth that real people do not live in Washington, it is quite common to talk to fourth- and fifth-generation Washingtonians who could not imagine living in any other city. When asked how Washingtonians feel connected to the city, many talk about community and neighborhood relationships. Washington is historically a city of black and white. Though Washington is becoming increasingly multicultural, it is still a city 66 percent African American and 27 percent white. It spills beyond its official boundaries into the neighboring states of Maryland and Virginia and is rich with the history of the Jewish community, German community, black community, newer immigrant communities, service and government workers, working class and wealthy, and generations of families.

Washingtonians have a special relationship with their city, where museums are free, national events are hosted on the Mall, and the president lives down the street—yet they were not able to vote for president until the 1964 election. Washingtonians can recall celebrating the Fourth of July on the Mall a few blocks from their homes, spending an afternoon at the National Zoo, and playing hide-and-seek in the Smithsonian museums after school. Living in Washington means the national news is the local news, and daily life intersects with events of national and international significance.

The *Growing Up in Washington* project has added new scholarship on the history of childhood by emphasizing the importance of place in the experience of children. The most common themes that were repeatedly echoed in memories of place were references to the importance of movie theaters to children and the impact of segregation. Often both segregation and movie theaters were mentioned in the same story, because segregation dictated where one could go in Washington. For Washingtonians born before 1954, segregation was a way of life with separate schools, separate theaters, and separate traditions. While white children went to the White House on Easter Monday for an egg roll, black children created an alternative tradition of visiting the Zoo—a tradition remaining to this day. Black Washingtonians careened through the air in roller coasters at Suburban

11

Gardens and white Washingtonians frolicked in the fun house at Glen Echo. All Washingtonians could venture downtown and walk by Woodie's, Murphy's, and Lansburgh's department stores, but black Washingtonians were not allowed to try on hats in Garfinckel's or eat a piece of Reeves strawberry pie at the counter. The Smithsonian Museums, the National Zoo, Griffith Stadium, the Central Public Library, and Rock Creek Park were notable exceptions in segregated Washington.

Growing Up in Washington provides a sampling of the experiences the children of Washington had over the past century. Together these memories weave a story of Washington and begin to show the nuances of living in different quadrants, in different neighborhoods, in different religious affiliations, and in different time periods over the past century. Part of growing up in the capital city is that the lives of ordinary people intersect with extraordinary events. Washingtonians share experiences about the Cadet Corps in the black and white schools, spending afternoons along the Tidal Basin beating the summer heat, attending presidential inaugurations, spending Saturdays at the movies, and riding the streetcars and buses. Every person who shared their story was thrilled to talk about the city of their childhood that they continue to call home.

Growing Up in Washington is a book of many voices and perspectives: Marion Jackson Pryde grew up in Shaw in the 1910s sheltered from the harsh realities of segregation; Markus Ring walked President Harding's dog and ate cookies at the White House; Richard Hawes played in the alleys of working class Northeast with all the neighborhood children; Loretta Carter Hanes could not understand why she had to walk extra blocks to a park when there was a park two blocks from her house where white children played; Damon Cordom, the son of Greek immigrants, learned to speak English on the playgrounds of the Weightman School in Dupont Circle during the Depression; Mary Barrick Stilwell and her friend Opal did not realize their interracial friendship was unusual in the 1960s; Keith Lofton took the bus across town from Southeast to Northwest to get to Francis Junior High everyday; Jacquelyn Joyner spent time playing in Judge Moultrie's office as a child while her father was working; and the memories go on. While reading *Growing Up in Washington*, you will meet Washingtonians of different races and religions from different quadrants of the city from ages 18 to 96 who are united by their mutual love of the city.

The immediacy of these stories provides a sense of the social and cultural changes in the city over the past 50 years. For residents, this book offers validation of their own heritage and personal memories and new opportunities to appreciate the life journeys of other Washingtonians. For people who grew up outside the city but are interested in learning more about Washington, the book offers a glimpse into the daily lives of Washingtonians and the unique, yet familiar experiences of childhood in the capital city. For those interested in urban history and American culture, excerpts and photos illustrate the evolution of the city as well as the changes in American culture over the past century. *Growing Up in Washington* offers insight into the people of Washington as well as the broader story of urban development, changes in American culture, and the growth of popular culture throughout the 20th century. More than a memory book for Washingtonians, *Growing Up in Washington* is a look into a city so many people know as a monumental seat of government, but few know as a thriving community of people.

MEETING THE CHILDREN

FLORA BLUMENTHAL ATKIN, born in 1919 to Joseph and Anna Levi Blumenthal, grew up around the Mount Pleasant and Columbia Heights neighborhoods playing with her younger sister Eleanor and beating the summer heat. Flora recalls a carefree childhood filled with hours of piano playing and dancing lessons. She attended Bancroft Elementary, Powell Junior High, and Roosevelt High Schools.

ERIN MARIE BARRINGER grew up in Friendship Heights picnicking around Rock Creek Park, dancing in recitals, and spending time with friends eating s'mores at Xando. Born in 1983, she has a brother five years younger. Their grandmother took them to museums, concerts, and theater around the city. Erin attended Aidan Montessori, the National Presbyterian School, and the National Cathedral School. Just graduating high school and about to leave the city for the first time, Erin already appreciates how special it is to grow up in the capital city.

SALLY LICHTENSTEIN BERK recalls the carefree days she enjoyed playing with her neighborhood and school friends. Born in

1945 to Harold and Betty Shapiro Lichtenstein, Sally is the oldest of three children. She attended J.G. Whittier Public Elementary, Wheaton Woods Elementary,

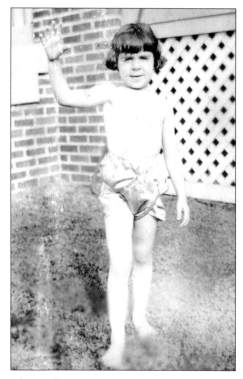

Flora Blumenthal Atkin in her backyard, c. 1926. (Courtesy Flora Blumenthal Atkin.)

13

Belt Junior High, and Peery High Schools. One of the first baby boomers, Sally spent her early years living on an army base and in an apartment building in Southwest before her family moved to Wheaton, Maryland with the help of the GI Bill.

SANDY BERK grew up in Northeast Washington playing World War II games and trading cards around Fort Totten, before moving to Wheaton as a teenager shortly after school desegregation. Samuel and Esther Berk had their second son, Sandy, in 1943, four years after the birth of their son Paul. Sandy attended Queen Elementary, McFarland Junior High, and Wheaton High Schools. Born during World

War II, Sandy recalls the growth in Washington in the postwar years.

CHARLES BROTMAN grew up in the Eckington neighborhood of Northeast Washington dancing the jitterbug and playing sports. Charlie was born in 1927 to Milton and Esther Brotman and lived with his sister and parents behind their family store, Mother's Market. He attended school near his house at Emery Elementary, Langley Junior High, and McKinley Technical High Schools.

Coming into the city on a regular basis for outings, **TIMOTHY BURTON** grew up a Washingtonian in suburban Maryland.

Charlie Brotman outside his home in the Eckington neighborhood, c. 1944. (Courtesy Charlie Brotman.)

Jo Forbes Carpenter on a pony in front of her Fessenden Street bungalow, 1931. (Courtesy Jo Forbes Carpenter.)

Robert and Mildred Beatty Burton had Tim and his twin brother, Tom, in 1951. Growing up in a Catholic household, the twins attended St. Mary's Elementary and Gonzaga High Schools.

JO FORBES CARPENTER grew up around Tenleytown riding the streetcars, shopping downtown at Woodward & Lothrop, and attending Senators games at Griffith Stadium. George and Rosina Forbes had their only child, Jo, in 1926. She attended Phoebe Hearst Elementary, Alice Deal Junior High, and Woodrow Wilson High Schools.

BREENA CLARKE COOPER was born in 1951 and grew up on 739 Madison Street, NW. She lived in a lively household with her parents, older brother Charles Payne, older sister Cheryl, younger sister Vicki, and great aunt Hannah Logan. Breena attended Truesdell Elementary, St. Gabriel's, and Immaculate Conception High Schools.

Breena and Vicki Clarke dressed for Easter, 1959. (Courtesy Breena Clarke.)

MARY MEADE COATES grew up around Capitol Hill in a close-knit community with neighbors who watched over and helped raise her. Born in 1931 to James and Viola Meade, Mary grew up in Southeast Washington on Carrollburg Place. Mary was 12 when her mother died of tuberculosis and her aunt moved into the house to help raise the family. She attended William Syphax Public, S.J. Bowen Public, Randall Junior High, and Dunbar High Schools.

DAMON CORDOM became a Washingtonian and an American while playing baseball in the alleys, learning English on the playgrounds, and going to the movies. Damon, born in 1932, was the first American in his family. His parents migrated from Greece in the 1920s to

Dupont Circle. Damon went to Weightman Elementary School, Force Public School, and St. Matthew's School. After his family moved to Cleveland Park, Damon attended Deal Junior High and Wilson High Schools.

JAMES DAVIS recalls growing up in Northeast Washington before and after segregation. Born in South Carolina in 1942, James moved to Washington when he was five years old. When James first arrived in the city, his family lived in different rooming houses on Capitol Hill before settling in the Deanwood area. He attended Lovejoy, Pierce, Carver, Kelly Miller Junior High, and Spingarn High Schools.

JUDY SCOTT FELDMAN says she couldn't imagine a better place to grow up than

15

Judy Scott Feldman, 1959. (Courtesy Judy Scott Feldman.)

Tracy Ferguson at four years old, c. 1975. (Courtesy Tracy Ferguson.)

3129 Westover Drive, SE, with a view of the Capitol and the monuments and with a neighborhood full of playmates. The middle child of five, Judy was born in 1952. Her mother, Mary, raised the children, and her father, Thomas, worked as the chief clerk of the Senate Appropriations Committee. Judy attended St. Francis Xavier and La Reine High Schools.

TRACY FERGUSON grew up in Chevy Chase, D.C., where she attended Beauvoir and National Cathedral Schools and enjoyed a close-knit extended family. Margot Dyson and James Felton Ferguson had Tracy in 1971 and brought her home to 5341 Nevada Avenue, NW. Her parents divorced shortly after her brother Albert was born, yet still remain friends and partners in parenting.

GEORGE FERRIS JR. was born in 1927 in Chevy Chase, Maryland, a few blocks from Washington, D.C., where he spent most of his childhood days. Because they considered schools in D.C. more competitive than those in Maryland, the Ferris parents sent their daughter Jean and son George to school in Washington. George attended Murch Public and E.V. Brown Public Schools before transferring to St. Albans School for Boys.

SUSAN TASSLER GINSBERG spent many days with her younger brother Alan in Meridian Hill Park and the National Zoo just a few blocks from their apartment house. Born in 1940, Susan grew up in Mount Pleasant before moving to Friendship Heights in 1954 as public schools were being desegregated. She attended H.D. Cook

Elementary, McFarland Junior High, and Wilson High School.

LORETTA CARTER HANES spoke of her childhood as a young African American in segregated Washington. The sixth child of Hattie Louise Thomson and Joseph Washington Carter, Loretta was born in 1926. Joseph was the first professionally trained black baker in Washington, and Hattie cared for their nine children. Loretta lived at 328 Bryant Street, NW in Shaw, a community of neighbors who watched over her. She attended Lucretia Mott Elementary, Shaw and Garnet-Patterson Junior High, and Armstrong High Schools.

RICHARD E. HAWES was born in 1923 at 217 R Street, NE in his childhood home—he didn't know anyone born in a hospital from his neighborhood. His family moved to a brownstone on 209 R Street, NE when Richard was just three years old and his sister Margaret Lee was five years old. Richard went to Eckington Elementary, Langley Junior High, and McKinley High Schools.

ISAAC COSBY HUNT III, known as Cosby, grew up in the 1970s and 1980s. The only child of Elizabeth and Isaac Cosby Hunt Jr., Cosby was born in 1971. The Hunts lived in Tiber Island in Southwest for four years before moving to the Hawthorn neighborhood in Chevy Chase. Cosby attended Murch Public and Lafayette Public Elementary Schools and St. Albans High School.

Susan Tassler Ginsberg having fun at the National Zoo, c. 1945. (Courtesy Susan Tassler Ginsberg.)

Loretta Carter Hanes posing at the Seventh and Rhode Island Avenue photo shop, 1944. (Courtesy Loretta Carter Hanes.)

Cosby Hunt and his new comic books on Christmas morning, c. 1977. (Courtesy Cosby Hunt.)

Kim Jones with her brother Eugene, c. 1975. (Courtesy Kim Jones.)

Playing around Howard University and fishing in the Tidal Basin, **FRANK R. JACKSON** was aware that Washington was a special place to grow up. Born in 1908 in Ledroit Park, his family moved to a large house near Howard University on Georgia Avenue and Fairmont Street, NW when he was three years old. His father was a waiter and his mother worked as a domestic in addition to raising their daughter and six sons. Educated under the segregated school system, Frank remembers a world-class education at Bruce Elementary and Dunbar High Schools.

MYLES MACCRIMMON JOHNSON grew up in the Burleith neighborhood, near Georgetown. Artists Wynne and Iris Johnson had their second son, Myles, in 1929. He went to Fillmore Elementary School, Gordon Junior High, and Western High School.

KIM JONES grew up in the Fairlawn neighborhood of Southeast, helping her grandmother run local civic groups and hanging out with her friends. Born in 1968, Kim was raised by her grandmother Thelma Jones, a local activist who taught her granddaughter about responsibility and self pride, while still allowing her to be a teenager. Kim attended Fletcher-Johnson and Roosevelt High Schools.

Growing up in Oxon Hill, Maryland just over the District line, **JACQUELINE JOYNER** spent her days playing in her neighborhood with her school friends as well as helping her father at his law offices downtown. The second child of James and Tricia McGee Joyner, Jacque was born in 1969. Her parents divorced when she was young, and Jacque moved to Los Angeles with her brother Brian and mother. Jacque and Brian returned to the D.C. area in 1977 to live with their father. She attended Flintstone Elementary, John Hanson Junior High, and Oxon Hill High Schools.

DOROTHY MARITA KING was born in 1908 and grew up around Howard University playing quietly in the neighborhood. Her father died at a very young age, so her mother supported the two of them as a domestic worker as well as a chef at the Kenesaw Apartments. They moved to Philadelphia for a few years when Dorothy was a teenager. She went to Garnet-Patterson-Phelps Elementary School and finished her last two years of high school at Dunbar High School, after returning from Philadelphia. Very light skinned, Dorothy passed in both the white and black community in segregated Washington.

Playing on the Mall and meeting influential Washingtonians were an everyday part of **AUSTIN KIPLINGER**'s childhood. W.M. and Irene Austin Kiplinger had their son in 1918. Austin's mother and sister Jane Ann moved back to his mother's hometown of Toledo, Ohio, when Austin was young. Austin spent most of his formative years living with either his father in Columbia Heights and Dupont Circle or his paternal grandparents near Lee Highway in Virginia. He attended Wilson Teacher's College for kindergarten, elementary, and junior high schools in Virginia, and then back to D.C. for high school at Western High School.

Growing up in a quiet neighborhood in Maryland, **GEOFFREY KOONTZ** came into the city for school fieldtrips and family outings on a regular basis. Wayne and Elizabeth Koontz had their son Geoffrey at Sibley Hospital in 1976. Geoffrey went to Montessori Country School and assorted

private schools before moving to Kensington in 1984. After the move he attended both Kensington Parkwood Elementary School and Walter Johnson High School.

LILLIE LATTEN grew up around U Street across from the old Children's Hospital. The middle of six children, Lillie was born in 1938. Her mother, Alice, worked in Children's Hospital and her father, Nathaniel, worked at Saks Furrier and General Services Administration. Lillie attended Harrison Elementary, Garnet-Patterson Junior High, and Cardozo High Schools. Attending elementary school during World War II, she recalls rationing and stamp books as well as the excitement of riding in a tank bought with the money collected from her elementary school.

Born in 1963, **DESMOND LEARY** is four years older than his sister. His parents divorced when they were young and the siblings spent their childhood years divided between the Brightwood neighborhood in Washington, D.C. living with their mother and Columbia, Maryland living with their father. In Maryland, Desmond went to Owen Brown Middle School and then Oakland School; in D.C., he attended St. Luke's Kindergarten, Brightwood Elementary School, Paul Junior High School, Roosevelt High School, and the School Without Walls.

ANDREA LITTLEJOHN grew up in the Manor Park neighborhood playing double dutch at Fort Slocum Park and kickball in the alleys with her friends. Four years younger than her brother, Andrea was born in 1962. Her father was a lab technician and her mother was a teacher in Mount Pleasant. She attended Rudolph

Florence Crawford Marvil in front of the Capitol, c. 1936. (Courtesy Florence Crawford Marvil.)

Marion Jackson Pryde at her home in the Shaw neighborhood, 1919. (Courtesy Marion Jackson Pryde.)

Elementary, Rabaut Junior High, and Hawthorne High Schools.

JANET KASDON LOBRED grew up during the Depression playing in the alleys in Friendship Heights and finding simple pleasures of childhood despite the devastating effects of the Depression on her family. Born in 1920 at Sibley Hospital, Janet spent her early years in Northeast before her family moved to upper Northwest. Janet attended E.B. Brown, Deal Junior High, Western High, and Wilson High Schools.

LEONARD LOBRED grew up on Ingleside Terrace in Mount Pleasant playing ball in the streets and building forts in Rock Creek Park. An only child, he was born in 1920. His father worked for the IRS and his mother was a substitute teacher and homemaker. Leonard attended Bancroft Elementary, Owl Junior High, and Central High School, on Thirteenth and Clifton, before it became Cardozo.

KEITH LOFTON grew up in Southeast Washington in the Park Naylor Apartments playing sports and music. The third child of Francine and Maurice Lofton, Keith was born in 1966. His parents divorced when Keith was little, and he lived with his mother. Keith attended Stanton Elementary, Francis Junior High, and Ballou Senior High Schools.

ALISON LUCHS grew up in upper Northwest, sledding down the hills on Appleton Street in the winter and playing in the nearby park in the summer. Born to Wallace Luchs Jr. and Barbara Bayer Luchs in 1948, Alison was the oldest of three children. She attended Ben Murch Elementary, Alice Deal Junior High, and Woodrow Wilson High Schools.

FLORENCE CRAWFORD MARVIL grew up around U Street in the Portner Apartment building. A white family in the heart of U Street was not typical, but Florence did not consider it unusual and loved where she grew up. George and Emilie Morrison Marvil had their second daughter, Florence, around 1925. She attended St. Paul's Catholic School, John Quincy Adams, Ross, and Central High School, which is now Cardozo High School.

MARION JACKSON PRYDE was born in 1911 and grew up in Shaw on the 1500 block of T Street, NW with her five brothers and sisters. Her father, Samuel, was a butler at the White House from the Taft to the Truman administrations and her mother, Eliza, raised their six children. Attending Sumner Elementary, Bell, and Dunbar High Schools, Marion participated in theater, music, and debating.

Tom Reese sledding down his front path at 1732 Massachusetts Avenue, SE, 1935. (Courtesy Tom Reese.)

Markus Ring standing with his cousin Gertrude Lachman, 1921. (Courtesy Markus Ring.)

TOM REESE was born in 1933 and lived in the Hillcrest neighborhood until 1939 when his family moved to Congress Heights. He had a great childhood in Congress Heights and then his family moved to Prince George's County, Maryland in 1948. He attended Stanton Elementary, Congress Heights Elementary, Kramer Junior High, Anacostia High, and Maryland Park High Schools.

MARKUS RING remembers his childhood exploits using the White House lawn as his playground. The fourth child of Nathan and Karoline Ring, Markus was born in November 1915. His father had migrated from Austria in 1892 and his mother from Germany as an infant. The family lived

above his father's shoe repair shop at 722 Seventeenth Street, NW, where Nathan proudly crafted shoes for prominent Washingtonians including presidents from Theodore Roosevelt to Franklin Delano Roosevelt. As a child, Markus attended Force Elementary School. His family moved to Petworth in 1924 and he attended the Petworth School, McFarland Junior High School, and McKinley Technical School.

GRETCHEN ROBERTS-SHORTER grew up in the Burrville neighborhood of Northeast, and in Northwest in LeDroit Park, Adams Morgan, and Brightwood. The older of two girls, Gretchen was born in 1946. Gretchen switched schools whenever the family moved, attending several schools including

Danny and his friends in their Star Trek shirts for his sixth birthday party, 1976. (Courtesy Danny Rose.)

Burrville Elementary School, H.D. Cooke Elementary School, Truesdell Elementary School, MacFarland Junior High School, and Roosevelt High School.

DANNY ROSE reminisced about growing up in an integrated neighborhood on Capitol Hill. Born in August 1970 to Nancy and Joe Rose, Danny spent his early years playing around Capitol Hill, where he attended Peabody Elementary School. His mother worked for the Department of Labor and his father ran Rose's Liquors and then opened Capitol Hill Records. In 1979 the Rose family moved to St. Thomas, Virgin Islands, and two years later, returned to the metropolitan area to Bethesda, Maryland. Danny attended Pyle Junior High and Whitman High School.

LARRY ROSEN played touch football in the alleys of Four and a Half Street, SW with the neighborhood boys. The youngest of four children, Larry was born in Wyoming in 1923. The family moved to Washington in 1927 when Moses Yoelson, Al Jolson's father, retired as a kosher butcher, opening the position for Larry's father, Arthur Rosen. The family moved to Yoelson's old house at 713 Four and a Half Street, SW. Larry went to S.J. Bowen Elementary, Greenleaf Elementary, Jefferson Junior High, and Central High Schools.

ROBERT ISRAEL SILVERMAN grew up in the Park View, Capitol Hill, and Columbia Heights neighborhoods where he played with his cousins. Morris and Annie Silverman, who were grocery store owners, had their middle child, and only son, in 1912. Skipping several grades in school, Robert attended Blair Elementary School and Business High

Twins Marvin and George Tievsky posing in Tenleytown, c. 1922. (Courtesy Marvin Tievsky.)

School, where he was a member of the Cadet Corps.

MARY TERESA BARRICK STILWELL was born around 1950 and spent her early childhood in Hyattsville, Maryland before moving to Brookland on Tenth Street, NE. She attended the Campus School of Catholic University and Academy of Our Lady High School. Mary recalls spending countless hours with her best friend Opal growing up around Catholic University in Brookland where she still lives today.

CLARA SHARON TAYLOR was born in 1925 in Warren County, North Carolina. Unable to make a profit off the land, her family moved to Georgetown in search of a better life in

Adam Vann before a soccer game, 1980. (Courtesy Adam Vann.)

1932. Clara attended Phillips Elementary School, Francis Junior High School, and Dunbar High School.

MARVIN TIEVSKY was born in 1917 in Brooklyn, New York and his family moved to Washington, D.C. when he was three. His father owned a grocery store at Seventeenth and Gales Streets, NE for four years before the Tievsky family moved to Tenleytown—a neighborhood his parents considered ideal for raising their twin sons and daughter. Marvin and his twin brother, George, attended the Henry T. Blow

Elementary School for three years, the newly built Bernard T. Janney Elementary School through eighth grade, and then Western High School.

ADAM VANN, who grew up in Potomac, Maryland, was born to Terry and Linda Vann in 1973. Adam's mother was a school nurse and his father was a lawyer for the National Labor Relations Board, working in an office near the White House where Adam was a frequent visitor. He attended Cold Spring Elementary, Robert Frost Middle, and Thomas S. Wootton High Schools.

THADDEUS MARCUS VERHOFF grew up in the Burleith neighborhood playing with his younger brother Zachary in Rock Creek Park and enjoying the local music scene. Gwendolyn and Dennis Verhoff had their first son, Thaddeus, in 1976. Thaddeus attended Stoddard Elementary School, Harding Middle School, and Woodrow Wilson High School.

HELEN COMBS WOOD grew up in Shaw on Twelfth and U Streets, NW. Her mother, Ellen Hawkins Combs, was a dressmaker for the Wilson White House and her father, Jacob Ross Combs, worked in the Pension Office. Ellen had three older sons from her first marriage before Helen was born in 1905. Helen attended Garnet-Patterson Junior High and Dunbar High School.

JOSEPH EUGENE ZEIS and his twin sister, Rosemary, were born in 1914 on the 500 block of Tenth Street, SW in an area called "the Flats." The Zeis family lived there for about ten years before moving to 422 Tenth Street, SW. Joseph attended Fairbrother Elementary, Jefferson Junior, and McKinley Technical High Schools.

1. Belonging to a Community

My mother sewed at home and was the dressmaker for the White House for the Wilson administration. There's a dress of hers in the Smithsonian worn by the second Mrs. Wilson. She worked for both the Mrs. Wilsons. The first one died and then he married Edith Galt and that's the one that turned in the dress to the Smithsonian. After Wilson was no longer president, Mama didn't go to the White House. They used to come to her. They used to send the limousine with the big insignia on it, and I can remember we moved to 1923 Thirteenth Street by then and the car pulled up there and Mr. Wilson was in the back of the car. I didn't see him. Mrs. Wilson came in to see Mama. She used to carry me up there to the White House. I can remember going up there. There was a room that they'd bring lunch to her. She used to bring little things home to us.

(Helen Combs Wood)

Washington was a strictly segregated city in every respect. When you are born into something, it's just natural and you become accustomed to it. If it were afflicted upon you all of the sudden, you would feel it more. As I got older it bothered me. I just didn't have sense enough to realize it was happening when I was younger. Washington was all I ever knew. Glen Echo was the big amusement park, but there was an amusement park called Suburban Gardens, which was black owned, black operated, and black patronized in Deanwood. Even the playgrounds were segregated. Once in awhile us kids would go into a white playground and have a little fun quickly. Mott School was strictly for black children and there were several black kids in the area. Their parents did all types of work activities. Lots were domestic workers and some worked in government services.

(Frank R. Jackson)

There were no restaurants you could attend unless they were black owned. My mother was careful to protect us and to keep us from being embarrassed. I wanted to go to this restaurant because I saw this salad advertised and she said "Oh that is a fine salad, but let's wait until we get home because it will cost us twice as much [to buy]." She went home and bought everything that was in that salad—the tomatoes, the lettuce, the pickle, the hard-

African-American children played in the playground behind the Lucretia Mott School in Shaw. (Courtesy Wymer Photo Collection, HSW Collections.)

boiled eggs, and everything that was on that plate in the window—and she fixed up a grand salad so that I didn't feel denied.

(Marion Jackson Pryde)

This was a very segregated town and a Southern town. There were so many things they wouldn't let the minorities participate in. We couldn't go to any of the big concerts downtown. The churches provided most of the cultural activities for us. I remember Marian Anderson sang at our church before she became famous and then, of course, there was the incident at the Lincoln Memorial. I remember my older sister taking me there to hear it and that was

great. She was on her way to greatness when she sang at our church, but she hadn't achieved status yet.

(Marion Jackson Pryde)

I attended Shiloh Church on L Street, NW between Sixteenth and Seventeenth Streets. We enjoyed it because they always had a Christmas celebration and Easter exercises and they had a bazaar there in the early years and we had Thanksgiving. The church provided most of the entertainment for us. Easter time we'd go to the Zoo rather than going to the White House. The Zoo was a favorite place. When the church wanted to have a picnic, they would reserve a section of the Zoo and that was

Marion Jackson Pryde sang in the choir and attended Shiloh Baptist Church on Ninth and P Streets, NW. (Courtesy Wymer Photo Collection, HSW Collections.)

always a treat. We brought a picnic and had the best of foods.

(Marion Jackson Pryde)

Synagogue on Fourteenth and Euclid. Tifereth Israel. We walked there. This was an Orthodox synagogue. I went to Hebrew school and got to be Bar Mitzvahed when I was 13. My mother and father had a big party for me.

(Robert Israel Silverman)

The Cadet Corps—this is the greatest thing that ever happened to me in my life. All I can say is here I was the captain. I have been meticulous about things all of my life and, in fact, that's what got me to be a

builder. I just talked to some guy today who said I built one of the finest houses in Washington. I paid attention to detail, detail, detail with every little thing and that carried over to the cadets. When you're in the cadets, it's like being in the Army or in the Marines. And incidentally they had a cadet camp that I went to in my last year of high school . . . We were in great order. We drilled two days a week, Mondays and Thursdays. We wore white gloves. We had to have our gloves clean and our shoes shined and our hair neat and all of those things as part of our training. You had to have your thumb the right way. That attention to detail may seem ridiculous, but it carried over to life. That's what I did

27

with the high school cadets, and when I did my homework, I'd do it all. You had to have good grades to be a cadet and have a liking for it. I was a corporal at the end of my first year. You had seven men, eight men in the squad. You had a front right and a rear right and they were my responsibility. That was my job. My second year I was a sergeant, and my third year I became a first sergeant. That was a very important job and I got a saber. I didn't have to carry a heavy rifle and for kids those rifles were heavy, very heavy. Cadets attracted so many, so many wonderful kids into the Cadet Corps who have all become no matter what they did, the classiest guys who came out of high school.

(Robert Israel Silverman)

I was active in Boy Scouts. We used to go camping and on day trips. That was interesting. At that time we went to the Third and C Streets, NW Boys Club. I was in the Scout organization about four or five years, mostly junior high ages. You had to be 12 years old. I'm not sure Cub Scouts were around then. It was quite involved in that we'd go on hikes every Sunday to nearby areas that weren't built up, like the Randall Highlands across the Anacostia River. We used to hike back there. We used to hike near Chain Bridge near the Virginia side up in the woods there.

(Joseph Eugene Zeis)

Social activity in those days centered around the old Jewish Community Center at Sixteenth and Q Streets, NW. It was there that I joined a group of fellows in a sort-of fraternity known as Sigma Delta. We met Saturday evenings at the Center for basketball and swimming, and maybe

Business High School's Company E Cadets Sullivan, Pieresma, Silverman, Settle, and Bowen at attention, 1928. (Courtesy Helen White Photo Albums, HSW Collections.)

The Jewish Community Center on Sixteenth and Q Streets, NW. (Courtesy Wymer Photo Collection, HSW Collections.)

movies later in the evening. The group met again on Sunday afternoons and participated in debates with other clubs. It was at this time that I met my future wife, Erma Martin.

(Markus Ring)

I was 19 when [I] graduated college and lived at home. I dated, but because I was Jewish, I only dated Jewish. Georgetown had a large Jewish community and then there was the Jewish Community Center at Sixteenth and Q. There was a Jewish Boy Scout troop at the JCC, which lasted until the 1960s. I was a boy scout until I was 16. I got as far as star but not an eagle scout. Next step was life and then eagle, but I got interested in girls by then.

(Marvin Tievsky)

Washington was different. If you were white and middle class, the only black people you

met were in labor or domestic service. You knew there were others, but you didn't meet them. Washington was different. You were aware that Washington had a black intelligentsia and the most highly educated black community in the country, but it was only later that you got to know them.

(Austin Kiplinger)

I lived in Northwest, but the people were prejudice and they'd call us names because we were Jewish and they would taunt us. They called us Jew baby and they were kind of ignorant.

(Janet Kasdon Lobred)

There was a little one-room schoolhouse where the black children went when I was at Deal. It didn't seem very fair that we had this new school. I could feel segregation, because my relatives lived in black areas and their customers were all black. I had

29

Florence Crawford Marvil attended services at the National Presbyterian Church at Thirteenth and New York Avenue, NW, 1928. (Courtesy Bishop Photo Collection, HSW Collections.)

the chance in the grocery stores to know the people.

(Janet Kasdon Lobred)

I knew my way on Sixteenth Street. Connecticut Avenue was the other side of the tracks. The park was a big divider, economically and socially, in my perspective. As a child I thought of them as two different worlds. I know my way on that side of the park and downtown. We could hear the lions roar and we spent time at the Zoo. This was our monumental city and I knew that area to the Capitol and the Library of Congress. The Supreme Court building was being built when I was a kid. I rode the streetcar to Lincoln Park. I had more confidence on the streetcar than on the bus.

(Leonard Lobred)

All the activity focused out front in the evenings. Half of the houses on the other side of the street had porches and everyone came out to the porches in the evenings. Kids congregated around lampposts. There were two lampposts. One was near the corner near the corner grocery store, DGS, which was part of the District Grocery Store chain. In the evening, especially in the summer, spring, or fall there was much activity out front. Girls played hopscotch or jump rope and boys pushed each other, and there were always things going on. Older boys and girls were flirting around the lampposts. There was always someone out who said, "I'll tell your mother." We hated it because people knew everyone's business, but it was kind of like an extended family.

(Richard E. Hawes)

New York Presbyterian Church downtown. I was always impressed that the men who seated you were always dressed in formal clothes and the ladies wore white gloves and hats. I was probably three years old then and always remember that. I have gone to the Presbyterian Church all my life and continue to go . . . I sang in the choir and practiced twice a week and sang on Sunday mornings at church. I had the worst singing voice you could imagine, but it was fun. I was in plays and in the choir. I went to Sunday school . . . I still know some of the people down there that I have known all of my life. It has been a community experience in Washington, but I've cherished knowing so many different ethnic groups that I've known from grade school and high school and I have friends of many descriptions.

(Florence Crawford Marvil)

We were separate and knew we were separate. We could use the libraries but we could not try on clothes or hats in stores. Because you were black you could stand on the bridge, but not sit on the steps to listen to concerts or watch fireworks near the Capitol. In 1933 you could listen to the concerts, but not sit on the steps. It was a way of life that you don't realize until you are older.

(Clara Sharon Taylor)

We had fun and were happy and didn't realize all the bad things. It took very little to be happy. We might walk down to the water or up Q Street and see the houses or walk by the stores on M or Wisconsin. Most of the fun was just being with friends. We would get a soda at People's and window shop and it was fun. We skipped rope and played hopscotch.

(Clara Sharon Taylor)

Fourth and Bryant where I lived was all colored. North Capitol was all white and we couldn't go beyond that point. The playground on Fourth Street was for the black kids and the playground on Second Street was for the white kids. As a child I could not understand why I had to cross Fourth Street to go to my playground and why I couldn't go to the white playground. So one day I wandered into the Second Street playground and the white children stoned me and said, "Your dress is raggedy. Get out, get out, get out." I ran back home crying, because I could not understand how we were all there together but we couldn't share it.

(Loretta Carter Hanes)

We went up and down Seventh Street when we were older. [There was a] Hecht's. A Hahn's shoe store was right there on Seventh and K. Goldenberg's was our store. Hahn's had an x-ray machine to measure your foot, because you weren't allowed to return shoes and you couldn't try on clothes in most of the stores downtown from Florida Avenue to L Street. We couldn't go into Garfinckel's—not even black maids or mulattos. No, no. It made us feel very sad. Once you get exposed to other things, that's the only time you feel there is difference. Back in our own neighborhood things were great. Once we began to travel on the bus and the streetcar, we sat in the back.

(Loretta Carter Hanes)

We didn't travel too far from our house. Our playground was the Zoo—that tiny little reservoir where we played and rolled our Easter eggs and we congregated. The playground was where you got most of your community relations. The playground, the swimming pools, the churches, the

31

Alley dwellings behind the Lucretia Mott School in Shaw. (Courtesy Wymer Photo Collection, HSW Collections.)

Loretta Carter Hanes and her friend Ruth, 1943. (Courtesy Loretta Carter Hanes.)

schools were your areas. You knew you were confined and the police let you know it. That's why the U Street and Shaw area was so important to us because it was our little world where the shops and people and stores were.

(Loretta Carter Hanes)

In the summer we did a lot on the playground. We went to the Mott, Howard, and Banneker Playgrounds. There were professionals at every playground. We were lucky to be at Howard because those were the cream of the crop and they would teach us sports. My mother would teach us little dances and songs and I would do them. I couldn't wait to teach the children "Two steps forward. Two steps back. This is the ball and jack." I was always teaching the children something. We'd sing and play and I was always showing off. We were occupied and didn't have time to get into trouble.

(Loretta Carter Hanes)

Friends on Four and a Half Street. Eddie Friedman and Ted Shazz are still my friends after over 60 years. We used to play touch football in the alley. Also we had a Boys Club and the Nye House. I was a good ping-pong player, and when I was 15, I played in the semifinals of a tournament. There were a lot of alleys. The big thing I remember about Southwest is there was very little crime before World War II. Integrated neighborhood of Jewish, Greek, Italian, black. There was a Sanitary Grocery on Fourth and F. Mostly corner groceries. There was no fear and everyone helped each other. It seemed to be a different atmosphere.

(Larry Rosen)

Larry Rosen and Joseph Zeis lived near Four and a Half Street, SW. Lost to urban renewal in the 1950s, this street is now just a memory. (Courtesy Wymer Photo Collection, HSW Collections.)

33

Austin Kiplinger, Marvin Tievsky, Janet Kasdon Lobred, and Myles MacCrimmon Johnson attended Western High School. (Courtesy Wymer Photo Collection, HSW Collections.)

I felt I was the only Jew in elementary school. I was looked upon as different, almost as black, because both the blacks and Jews were seen as different. My athletic abilities and personality made me stand out, so I was different than the rest of the Jews in other people's eyes.

(Charles Brotman)

Playgrounds were very important to me. Our block overlooks the Western High School Stadium. In the summer the Department of Recreation ran summer camps out of the various high schools in their fields. So that was close by and they had a great program—archery, you could sit around and talk, and of course play games and arts 'n crafts. It was a camp run by the city recreation. My friends went too.

(Myles MacCrimmon Johnson)

Washington was very segregated. There were a number of black families who lived in Georgetown. Many of the houses have since been gentrified. Anacostia was mainly a very white and a racist, Southern, redneck enclave, so it's very ironic that it has become a black enclave. One was aware that the city was divided. When I was older and I got into jazz, I went to Seventh Street where they had good music stores with records. Jazz, for me, was an awakening to what had happened to African Americans in our society, and it changed all that as far as I'm concerned. Jazz was an awakening for me. It made me more anti-racist than my parents were. My parents weren't racist, but they grew up in a culture with certain assumptions. Although I was always taught to respect people, they certainly didn't look askance at what I was doing.

(Myles MacCrimmon Johnson)

We went to the National Zoo all the time. Easter Monday and other times too. We didn't have access to a lot of places. We were kind of guided, sheltered, protected and didn't do a lot of exploring on our own. We knew there were places we couldn't go. We knew that by instinct because we didn't go. Your parents guided you in the right direction so you wouldn't get in trouble.

(Mary Meade Coates)

[I lived in a] close-knit neighborhood close to Capitol Hill. We knew the Capitol was there, but we had no dealings with it from day to day. We had our own separate lives— our own stores, our own businesses. We used to call our block the "village" because everybody told you what to do. We used to say we'd be glad when we grew up so we could get away from this village and pretty much do what we wanted to do. Everybody could tell you what to do. It was really like family. They looked out for my mother when she was sick so my father could go to work. He was a mechanic. He only went up to fourth grade, but could fix anything that moved.

(Mary Meade Coates)

We used to have concerts down on the waterfront down near the Watergate. I don't think we ever went down front. We sat up high, because you could see better. If you didn't get there early, early, early you didn't get a seat anyway. We sat on the top row in the back or stood. There's so much here to do free. So many things, it's amazing. It is a public city. I didn't take advantage of that as much when I was younger. You could hear concerts and things. We went to the monuments. We took advantage of some.

(Mary Meade Coates)

Lansburgh's and Hecht's were the downtown stores. Some of them we couldn't even try on clothes and we couldn't afford them anyway. So we stuck to where we knew we could try clothes on and what was comfortable. You came across some good people when you knew that was the rule that made some exceptions. One saleswoman wouldn't let me try on a hat, but let me take it and return it if it didn't fit, and she wrote the slip up as something else.

(Mary Meade Coates)

We had segregated neighborhoods and schools. Anacostia was all white at the time. Black people lived from Howard Road to St. Elizabeth's Hospital and from there it was all white to the District line. There was no high school for black kids in Anacostia, so they had to cross the river. They had

The National Zoo. (Courtesy Wymer Photo Collection, HSW Collections.)

Going downtown on F Street, NW. (Courtesy Wymer Photo Collection, HSW Collections.)

Cardozo, Armstrong, and Dunbar, and they had to travel a long way to school. We were very segregated. School integration changed the city forever.

(Tom Reese)

We were a middle-class family. My mother, Alice, worked at Children's Hospital. I grew up in 2206 Twelfth Place, NW in front of old Children's Hospital on W Street. I remember the day the Lone Ranger came to Children's Hospital and all of us gathered around and this happened in 1945 or '46. Back then Children's Hospital had all sorts of entertainment and they would sit outside on W Street. Back then it wasn't too many colored children—just white. But we always got to attend, because we lived right in front of Children's Hospital.

(Lillie Latten)

I remember when the bread man used to bring the bread around the corner of Twelfth and W to the Market on the corner. They had two little boys who were Jews and they used to come to our house and play with us all the time and play football all the time. Martin and Bobby. They used to play with us and used to have birthday parties and we used to go around to the market to the store for parties all the time. Those were the only white Jew boys there around at the time. They lived atop the store. As they grew, they moved away.

(Lillie Latten)

I was a member of the YMCA. My mother needed a place for me to go, especially in the summers. I started there when I was about eight. That was a very good experience in my life. Part of our ritual was to go to Banneker Junior High School and that's where we went swimming and we played. From the Y we were introduced to overnight camp—those were nice experiences. I met some of my first friends at the Y. With the Y we visited many places downtown. We learned to fish at the Tidal Basin—that was a regular ritual. We would virtually run up the monument several times. A large part of the Y was physical fitness. We'd go camping and do a lot of stuff outside. The Smithsonian was there, and not in the way it is today. We didn't do a lot of that with my family. Family time was more parks and church and to visit family members. At that time public access was not available to black folks, so we didn't have a lot available. A lot of things you might have been able to do, you didn't because you didn't feel welcome . . . and you didn't even have the whole area available even if you could go.

(James Davis)

My father is James A. Davis and my mother is Elvira Davis Grady. My father was a skilled craftsman for the Printing Office after World War II and my mother was a domestic for the most part, which was typical of the work [available] for African-American women. My father worked in a very segregated environment and my mother worked in a store she couldn't even shop in. Julius A. Garfinckel's was the Nordstrom's of that day. She couldn't shop in any of the stores. I remember a five and dime store called Kresge's where you could buy food, but you couldn't sit down. There was a lot of that in the city.

(James Davis)

When I first arrived in Washington and got acclimated to the area, I remember some semblance of social integration. The streets where I lived—Fifth, D, and F—were all

Tom Reese on a pony in the Hillcrest neighborhood of Southeast Washington—a common type of child's photograph in Washington, 1938. (Courtesy Tom Reese.)

very much integrated neighborhoods. We just didn't go to school together. During the day, very definitely, everybody played the usual childhood games together. Throwing balls, stickball, hopscotch, and other children's game. It was only at the time of desegregation in 1954, that there was a mass exodus from the city. I remember the last white family that left F Street—they had the house on the corner. Interestingly enough with gentrification that house was the first to be bought by a white family. I wanted to make the point that there was integration and children played together and adults talked together, but when it came to public access, that did not take place until after 1954.

(James Davis)

Richard Mansfield and Boys Club members, including Herbert Haas, Eugene O'Neil, and Bobby Derwin, c. 1943. (Courtesy Richard Mansfield Collection, HSW Collections.)

James Davis lived and played around Stanton Park—an integrated neighborhood in the 1940s and early 1950s. (Courtesy HSW Collections, CHS 2803.)

The neighborhood was changing and some moved out to the suburbs or Sixteenth Street to the ritzier areas. By '57 and '58 the neighborhood was changing rapidly. My family moved to the Wheaton/Rockville area in Maryland in 1957. Otis Drive in Rockville. Transition was hard because a lot of my friends moved to Sixteenth Street or Silver Spring and this was a different area. Most of the [old] street was Jewish, about 90 percent. We thought we were the majority, but to move to a more WASP area was a change. We were now about 15 percent Jewish. When I went to Belt Junior High, I was always referred to as a "Jew boy," which I had never heard before. Because my whole neighborhood was the same, I never knew I was different or inferior. This was a shock to know I was inferior.

(Sandy Berk)

I remember parks more when we moved to Adams Morgan and I started at H.D. Cooke

Elementary. I remember being near the Zoo. We could actually hear the elephants and tigers at night. It was kind of eerie and kind of fun all at the same time. 2525 Ontario Road. My sister was older and went to Cooke too, so that provided continuity. I remember the Zoo. We walked our dog at Meridian Hill Park. My grandmother was a seamstress and she cared for us during the day. She went to Meridian Hill with us.

(Gretchen Roberts-Shorter)

As a family we went to the park in Adams Morgan near Columbia Road and I remember going there. They had swings and playground equipment and a big grassy area. We went to Rock Creek Park a few times, but not as many child-oriented activities growing up—more family-oriented activities. We had two sets of cousins that lived within two blocks, so lots of visiting. At that point we all played together. When we were a little older we walked to Coolidge High to swim in the pool. That was fun having four female friends that were relatives. We visited each other's houses on Christmas morning. It was a big deal when we didn't believe in Santa anymore. It was a domino effect. My sister was the first to have that revelation. She saw the boxes of our presents and she broke the news to me. I was devastated. I remember picnics, birthdays, Christmas, all at houses.

(Gretchen Roberts-Shorter)

We went on tours in school. We went to the Capitol in school and I remember getting to shake hands with Sam Rayburn. We would go to symphony concerts at Constitution Hall. We'd go to the National Gallery, which is where I work now. At the time I remember being desperately bored and thinking when I grow up I won't have to come here anymore. The best thing about it was the building. I remember they said watch out for the slippery marble

floors and I remember thinking that was exciting. I think the docents in those days weren't as good as they are today. I got excited about Rembrandt, because he was the first artist in which I could understand the idea of style and creating. Otherwise it was boring. I didn't like Grumpy Old Saint Georgia the dragon much because the colors were bad . . . I took informal art when I was younger in school and at camp. I painted and did watercolors and dabbled, but I was never very good at it. I dabbled in every type of craft at camp.

(Alison Luchs)

The civil rights march was at the end of my freshman year. It was supposed to have changed the world. Brookland was mostly white. Our original next-door neighbors moved and a lovely family moved in. My father got teased at work because a black family moved next door and were referred to as "blockbusters." Everyone in the

People's Drug Store on the corner of Eighteenth and Columbia Roads, NW, an area now known as Adams Morgan. (Courtesy Wymer Photo Collection, HSW Collections.)

Enjoying a visit to the Tidal Basin and the view of the Jefferson Memorial, c. *1940. (Courtesy of Zack Spratt Collection, HSW Collections.)*

neighborhood was concerned when the civil rights march occurred and when the civil rights bill was signed that people would just take over—and in my world there wasn't much to take over. If someone wanted to sit on my swing, it was a public swing in the playground. Nothing really changed in our world at all.

(Mary Teresa Barrick Stilwell)

We got milk delivered from Thompson's Dairy until the dairy closed. There was a lot of industry between North Capitol and Florida. I remember Thompson's closed when the teamsters struck. We never went out for milk until Thompson's closed. Someone came to our door with baked goods. You could pick your doughnuts and your bread. It was wonderful. Mr. Falconi was the bakery guy and we had several milkmen, but our favorite and the last one

was Ford Wolpin. He went into computers when the dairy closed. It would have been better if these services still existed, but now the 7-11 is on the corner and open all the time.

(Mary Teresa Barrick Stilwell)

The Catholic Church was very good about integration. There weren't a lot of black students, but they were there. As far as I knew, we got along well and there weren't any big problems. The Catholic Church did try to be moral and teach ethics. They taught us to judge people based on their character and nothing else.

(Timothy Burton)

In the second week of our summer vacation we used to go around and behave pretty much as tourists in Washington. We went to the Smithsonian Museum of

Natural History. Of course that was just wonderful. We were three girls and we would dress up in our summer tourist outfits—white shorts, white blouses, and fresh tennis shoes. We would get fresh tennis shoes for the second week vacation. We would get either a blue or a red pair, and a white pair for when we went to the museum. We would have on our white tennis shoes, our white shorts, and our white blouses. That was important because there was an idea that when you went to downtown Washington you were supposed to be dressed and circumspect. That had to do with just the custom at the time and with your perception in the public as an African American. We had our hair neatly done, no loud laughing, and no goofing off especially in that part of town. But we

Cheryl, Breena, and Vicki Clarke in front of their house on Madison Street, 1957. (Courtesy Breena Clarke.)

would have a good time. The Natural History Museum was so exciting especially with the big elephant. He was wonderful. He is wonderful.

(Breena Clarke Cooper)

We went to the National Gallery of Art. I remember it was so beautiful with all that marble and it was so cool. This was also perfect for the summertime because those marble buildings were so cool. Long before air conditioning those marble places were some of the coolest buildings to be around in the summer. We did a lot of car trips to Hains Point. Oh god, we loved Hains Point. We'd just drive down there and park, get out, run around, and go down to the river edge. Of course, they had some swings and sliding boards in another area. We used to run over there. They had another area where they sold ice cream. See, as I recall back in that era, people didn't do as much eating at any opportunity. You know a lot of kids now can have six or seven ice cream cones a day. We couldn't just beg and wheedle for things all the time. My mother wouldn't allow it. We had certain things that we were allowed, so when we went on a trip to Hains Point we could have ice cream down there or we could wait and drive out to this ice cream parlor in Northeast. We couldn't do both.

(Breena Clarke Cooper)

The one thing that I think was so courageous of my parents was that in the face of these vestiges of segregation, they were still able to have a good time and a good life. They kept us from feeling embittered as young people. I guess they thought there was time enough when we got older. We really didn't realize the extent to which segregation limited our options until we were much older. Our parents

Careening down the roller coaster at Glen Echo, the white amusement park, c. *1940. (Courtesy HSW Collections, CHS 1056.)*

were sort of the buffers against it. I think that kind of thing is very courageous.

(Breena Clarke Cooper)

Another place I remember from my childhood, a particularly painful memory, was Glen Echo Amusement Park. We would drive out there and I can remember driving past and seeing the Ferris wheel and the roller coaster at Glen Echo and asking to go

and wanting to go. My mother would explain that we were not welcome there. I think she characterized it more in that way that we were not welcome there so we wouldn't want to go someplace where we weren't welcome. That was the best way to explain it to children. It was very sad and I can remember questioning her on why on earth would anybody not want us to go. We were nice kids. Why wouldn't they want us to go? It was some years later when we finally did get to go in and it was nice . . . maybe not quite as wonderful as we thought it would be, but it was nice.

(Breena Clarke Cooper)

Summer nights we would sit on the porch and read comic books. I would read everything. When our neighbors were done with theirs they would give them to us . . . We would read the same comics we read three days before. I also read Nancy Drew and played hopscotch. At night we sometimes had roller skating parties in our backyard. It was a very small yard and my parents decided to brick it up so it would be more useable as we got older. My dad put in floodlights and a basketball hoop and we would play basketball or have skating parties and my mom would make popcorn.

(Judy Scott Feldman)

I lived four blocks from the elementary school. My brother was four years older than me. Until he graduated, he would walk me to school and then when he graduated, I would walk with my neighborhood friends. There were crossing guards at the time. I would walk down First Street and take a right on Longfellow Street until I came to Second Street, NW and walk along Second and Longfellow to Second and Missouri Avenue and there was a crossing guard, because it was a busy thoroughfare. I crossed Missouri Avenue to Hamilton Street to Abraham, and school was there. We would play on the playground in warmer months until our teachers escorted us in. The playground was broken up into different areas for different teacher's classes. I knew the exact spot where I needed to go to see my classmates and we had to line up single file

when my teacher came to get us. We didn't have to wear uniforms. 1968 to 1973 I was in elementary school. Platform shoes were in style and as early as fourth grade I begged my mom to get me some. She didn't want to, but she finally broke down. Platform shoes and bellbottoms; Tom Jones shirts, which had large collars and poofy sleeves which you would see on the Brady Bunch or the Partridge Family; cornrows or Afros were in style. I had my hair chemically straightened, because my mom didn't want to deal with taking care of my hair . . . I wore dresses in elementary school until I dressed myself more in fifth grade. She got my dresses in second-hand stores and she handwashed them, because she was afraid they were fragile because they were older. I got to wear pants later.

(Andrea Littlejohn)

I remember us campaigning for Dixon for several years. I suppose that my family just decided to take some step in deciding how the community must come together. I don't remember how they got involved, but I suppose it has something to do with the feeling of black power going through black neighborhoods at that time. I remember going on marches . . . I remember going door to door for Dixon. Those are some of my earlier memories of participating.

(Keith Lofton)

Go out and see and there are people who don't look like you and don't speak like you. This is a town of many languages, styles, purposes, and ways. A person who lives in Washington, D.C. is very key to the world's goings on, the nation's goings on, the city's goings on. I see D.C. in comparison to London, Paris, Tokyo, and these are all international cities. And by the

Kim Jones grew up in Anacostia, c. 1973. (Courtesy Kim Jones.)

Jacque Joyner smiles for the camera, 1969. (Courtesy Jacque Joyner.)

'80s, when I was growing up, D.C. became a multicultural, multiethnic, multi-purpose denizen of business and humanity. I never see D.C. as my little community. Washington in my time is as famous as New York, if not more famous. Many people who experience Washington just experience the city as the Smithsonian and that's not the city. It's like an obligation to all see the Washington Monument, but not everyone can say they lived here.

(Keith Lofton)

I didn't go to the Washington Monument until I was 17 years old. I didn't appreciate the fact that we lived in the seat of government of the free world for a long time. People from outside the city appreciate it so much more than the African-American community who grew up in Washington. And this city is run by so

many African Americans and we took that for granted or didn't know. I have friends from college that were amazed when they saw a black teacher, and I didn't have a white teacher until high school. That's how it was. My mayor was black and everyone around me was black and we all just took it for granted. The first time I identified with being a Washingtonian was when I went to college. So many people are awed by the city and I never realized how incredible it was. I was from Chocolate City, but I had never before come to the realization that I was really a Washingtonian.

(Kim Jones)

My grandmother was virtually every officer within the Fairlawn area, the Citizen's Association in Anacostia, and the Anacostia Friends of the Library. We used Friends of the Library to reach out to children in the

45

Danny Rose's confirmation class in front of Temple Shalom, 1985. (Courtesy Danny Rose.)

area. Even now when she picks my son up from school, he goes to meetings and passes out flyers. We are intimately involved with so many grassroots organizations. My grandmother pulls you in through "Hey, what are you doing today?" and then gets you to do stuff for her. We used to do an information day parade through Friends of the Library. I always was the young voice giving suggestions about activities. It is the same core group of women in both organizations. I was president of Friends for three years after Northeastern and before law school.

(Kim Jones)

I am glad I grew up in Washington when I did. I feel good that I got to take for granted being black. I didn't have those same pressures of not being able to fit in because I was black. If nothing else, my identity as an African American was very secure growing up here. It's incomparable and

there is no place else African Americans can grow up as secure as I did. It was great for one thing, but in other ways it didn't prepare me for things I had to encounter later.

(Kim Jones)

In L.A. the circle of friends that I hung around were not very nice people. The people I met in D.C. were very nice and very straight-laced, very warm and very inviting and that's why we stayed friends. I didn't even search these friends out. They literally walked up to me in the playground and said, "Come play double dutch with me," and that's how I met them. I didn't even know how to jump double dutch, but they taught me and that's how I met them, Lisa and Tracy. I had a third best friend I met in the fourth grade, Tanya. The people I met in D.C. were warmer and more group oriented [than in L.A.]. I remember being teased a lot in L.A. It was brutal and then I got to D.C. and it was a lot warmer. I think it has to do with the Southern mentality. It was just a lot warmer. People made friends easily and you kept your friends.

(Jacqueline Joyner)

My parents were part of a group that much later would have been called yuppies, affluent people who were very young with disposable income. But they chose on purpose to move into an integrated neighborhood and to send their children to public schools. It really was integrated on the block . . . When we were in elementary school, we were all together. That was something special that we could have that interaction.

(Danny Rose)

We belonged to Temple Shalom. I got Bar Mitzvahed there. Some kids had been in Hebrew School for years, but I came in late. I was 12 when I got there. I took

Confirmation classes. I didn't feel like I had much in common with these kids from the suburbs. I did feel the Bar Mitzvah prep was good, and going to services together as a family.

(Danny Rose)

I went to Pyle Junior High and Whitman High, but I kept my friends from Peabody Elementary in D.C. I thought they had a much cooler life in D.C. than I did in the suburbs. My friends who stayed in the city in some ways seemed more racist than I did because they kept having bad encounters with kids from bad neighborhoods. By high school my friends had much stronger relationships with people of color. That didn't happen much in Bethesda.

(Danny Rose)

[It's a] remarkable city assuming there is a typical American way to grow up. Being in Washington creates a particular kind of

Danny Rose outside his Capitol Hill home with friends, 1979. (Courtesy Danny Rose.)

experience specific to the place. If you grew up in Manhattan you would have your own experiences. It is a good place to grow up to be politically savvy later. You get connected to politics. I remember when we lived on the Hill my parents kept chopping down the no parking signs for the Nixon inaugural. They kept taking them down when new ones were put up. Many in Capitol Hill did that if they hated Nixon.

(Danny Rose)

We were so family oriented. In the summers my cousins from L.A., California would come. Shari was my age, Christi was Albert's age, and Carla was a year below them. We all went to Town & Country, a day camp in Wheaton, Maryland. It had all the activities like swimming, horseback riding, archery, gymnastics—that was my favorite—and fencing. We went every summer. The summers gave us, the then youngest generation of a Washington family, the chance to get together for a minimum of three months a year in the city where multiple generations of our family had lived. Summers were so wonderful because everybody was here. We would often hang out in the "Terrace" [our grandmothers' house] and tumble in the yard, put on skits, or just sit and watch TV. One of our favorite things was to slide down the laundry shoot. The laundry shoot went from the third or fourth floor down to the basement. Only Christi had the guts to do it, and when she did we were all so envious and awe struck. It was hysterical.

(Tracy Ferguson)

I had this project in seventh grade for Medieval History and the project was to do your family crest. When I came home

Tracy Ferguson and her Washington and California cousins. (Courtesy Tracy Ferguson.)

with that assignment my mother flipped. I mean literally flipped. She said, "That's horrible. I can't believe you're doing that project. Not everyone has a family crest." And I said, "Ferguson is a Scottish name." My father told me it was Scottish and he showed me the family shield. My father said, "Let me help you draw this." It has three boors' heads and a buckle and I knew the colors and everything. My mom said, "Why don't you just tell her it's a slave owners name and that's how she got it." I could tell that my father was upset that my mother had said that in front of me, but he did not deny it. I remember I was so upset that I didn't do it that night because I had two people that loved me saying stuff like that and I didn't know how to process it. I didn't want people to see my color first, because I didn't.

(Tracy Ferguson)

A lot of my friends were from the city. I had friends from high school that lived in my neighborhood. I had a friend from Reston and one in McLean, Virginia. We would tease them both to death. We would say, "When's your jet coming in?" Anyone who lived in Virginia would get teased, at least Maryland wasn't separated from D.C. by a river. To us, albeit ridiculous, Virginia seemed almost like a different country, with a different culture and way of life. The poor Virginia folks got teased a lot. The Maryland folks didn't . . . There are certain things people growing up in D.C. have in common. They are either a "Virginia sympathizer" or "Maryland sympathizer." Another very D.C. thing is that if you are asked by another Washingtonian, "Where did you go to school?" they will respond with the name of their high school.

(Tracy Ferguson)

Tracy Ferguson dressed for graduation from the National Cathedral School, 1990. (Courtesy Tracy Ferguson.)

Single-sex education was great. It wasn't uncool or unladylike to be smart, outspoken, or aggressive when need be; it was expected. The only problem is that outside of school and as I got older, I noticed that sometimes people did not judge me by my personality or level of intelligence but my appearance. I wish people saw me as Tracy first, the way I did. One of the great things about growing up in Washington is that it is a place where the concept of the "monolithic black" does not, cannot, exist. There are black people from all different economic stratas, of various educational levels, shades, and some that are combinations of multiple races, ethnicities, and cultures. It's wonderful! The one bad thing, was that as a child from Northwest Washington, I tended to stay in

Adam Vann at Cabin John with his brother Brian (on left) and friends Scott and Erik Zimmer (on right), 1981. (Courtesy Adam Vann.)

My father worked at the Pentagon during the Carter administration. That was the coolest and the biggest office building in the world. Little boys are usually fascinated with military stuff so this was cool because this is what controls the planes and ships. He took me to "the mess," which was the eating room of the Pentagon. It was a big deal. I will never forget him taking me down the halls of the Pentagon and showing me all these different paintings. There was a painting with a soldier looking through binoculars and as you walked down the hallway, the binoculars followed you.

(Cosby Hunt)

Northwest and wasn't very familiar with the other three of the city's quadrants. So, while I had an idea of all that Washington had to offer, I tended have my experiences in only a part of a much larger city.

(Tracy Ferguson)

My mom and I would watch soap operas together in the summertime and we would watch the *Today* show together when she was picking through my Afro. I remember watching Bryant Gumbel, Jane Pauley, and Willard Scott while my head was flicking back. Then in high school, hands down my favorite show was *Moonlighting*. That was the only show I made sure I watched every time it came on. At one point I watched so much television when I was a kid that my mom put a moratorium on it.

(Cosby Hunt)

My dad worked until last year for the National Labor Relations Board as a staff lawyer. Now he works within government doing labor laws. I went to work with him sometimes. He had office toys on his desk for me. It was always exciting going down to his office. I liked going downtown. As a little kid there was something exciting about going downtown. The White House was right there and so I felt like we were next-door neighbors with the president. My mom would drive us down. Once I was past elementary school I don't remember going. Once I was older we didn't sit around his office while he worked.

(Adam Vann)

Being a kid you think your block is the end of the world and the local news is your news. Well, the local news really was the news here. If there was a report about anything, the reporters were either in Washington, D.C. or in New York, where my grandparents lived. It was reinforced that my universe was *the universe*.

(Adam Vann)

Music defined D.C. My neighborhood has an annual picnic that has been going on for years. The first year that it was put on, they got Mary Chapin Carpenter to play there. She was unknown at the time and playing for some dive bar in Georgetown every other night. That was before I was there. There were always bands.

(Thaddeus Marcus Verhoff)

Things were happening outside of school. I joined a Little League team. My dad was really into baseball. One of the first things he ever got me was a baseball glove. When he was in high school or college, he was drafted by the Baltimore Orioles but he went to the Peace Corps instead . . . I remember playing with my dad. He would hit grounders to me. He taught me how to throw a curve ball when I was 14, but he wouldn't let me throw one. He said this is how you do it, but you can't because you'll hurt your wrist. That was the kind of things we did . . . We were the Pirates Little League team. I remember when we got our uniforms it was like the happiest day of my life. It was just so awesome, and we had those mesh backed hats. It was great to have my own uniform. It had stirrups and I thought it was so cool. Getting a uniform in general might be special, like if you are in the Army or Marines—and when you are 12 or 13 this was great.

(Thaddeus Marcus Verhoff)

Growing up I took a metro bus to school. I remember taking the metro bus to school and I remember visiting my relatives and saying, "I ride the school bus" and they were shocked. "You ride a city bus to school?" "Yeah, it's really simple." You just put your token in and the bus driver had a lever to push all the coins down. After school the bus would wait behind Stoddard

and you'd play. Then he'd start the bus up and you'd hear it and he'd wait for us to run on the bus and he'd drive us all home again. The bus driver was pretty cool. He taught me how to start the bus. It was probably second or third grade when I started to ride the bus. I would chaperone my brother to school, too. You couldn't mess up the bus; it was so easy. It was like a block from my house. I walked down with my mom and this other kid would meet us. Sometimes my father would come down and I'd get on and say, "Good-bye Dennis. Good-bye Gwen," and they wouldn't say good-bye to me until I called them mom and dad. They were very insistent about that.

(Thaddeus Marcus Verhoff)

I got to ring the bells at the National Cathedral. I know it's a unique opportunity to ring a thousand-pound bell in such a famous cathedral.

(Erin Marie Barringer)

2. CELEBRATING HOLIDAYS

We went to the Zoo on Easter Monday. That was very popular. We would take a little picnic basket and go. Some of us went to the White House, but the Zoo was the most popular place, and it would be crowded with the people that you knew.

(Helen Combs Wood)

Christmas was usual. Christmas trees, toys, and Christmas dinner. We had turkey with all the trimmings—the dressing, the candied sweet potatoes, different vegetables. The turkey and the dressing were my favorite. I got a little brass bed for my doll. I got a desk and chairs. I always got clothing. I always got fruit. Apples and oranges. We always kept a fruit bowl on the table. Bananas, apples, and oranges. We always had nuts around the holiday season.

(Dorothy Marita King)

May Day was a big event in the Washington school system. They ask all the little girls to wear white and I remember one year the stores ran out of white dresses because all the little girls bought white dresses. We had the physical education teacher teach us games and dances. The street was blocked off and we had the program right on

Second Street when I was in Bell. There was a government building right across the street and I know the workers were standing at the window and not doing their work. They'd watch our rehearsal and want to know what day the actual performance took place and [their boss] would excuse them to watch our program. We'd wind the May pole. They tried to make it into a physical education program. They stressed good health. Child Health Day is what I think they called it rather than May Day—that was the emphasis. We had contests and the different schools had different things to celebrate. It was always the first of May and all the schools were doing their thing for that day. That day was special because each class had a program to perform, so it was a busy day.

(Marion Jackson Pryde)

My mother was cousin to Carter G. Woodson, the historian, and he always came to spend Thanksgiving and Christmas dinner with us. One of my first memories is of his being at the door. I opened the door for him at Christmastime and he had an armful of gifts all wrapped in white paper and tied in red ribbon. It was a book for

Breena, Cheryl, and Vicki Clarke dressed in white for the May Day procession, 1958. (Courtesy Breena Clarke.)

Flora Blumenthal Atkin dressed for the Purim parade at Adas Israel Synagogue, c. 1926. (Courtesy Flora Blumenthal Atkin.)

each of the children, for the most part they were books that he had written or were published by his company, Associated Publishers. Of course we still have those and I treasure them a great deal. That was a big enough celebration with six children, my mother and father, and Dr. Woodson. Of course we always had a Christmas tree and exchanged gifts with the family. Oranges were not plentiful, but we always had an orange in my stocking, which was quite a treat, and other little things like candies and nuts. Clothes were always a favorite and we got toys. I remember when the colored dolls first were made, but they were so expensive so my parents stuck with the regular dolls. Then there were games and I liked games better than dolls.

(Marion Jackson Pryde)

My father was Protestant and my mother was Catholic. My father converted and

so I was raised Catholic. We went to St. Dominick's Church at Sixth and E Streets, SW. I was christened and had first communion there. For Easter we dressed up in new clothes for church and then Easter Monday we went to the monument lot where we so-called rolled Easter eggs and there was a picnic. That was a get-together for the family. We frolicked on the monument grounds, which was a very popular spot. We never went to the White House, but we weren't too far from the monuments. We just walked there from where we lived.

(Joseph Eugene Zeis)

Washington, D.C. was a part of my life growing up. Easter Sundays and Sundays in general were important. We'd walk to what you'd call uptown and a lot of people were walking downtown, but we were walking uptown because we were south of that area. We were in easy walking distance and Sunday was a family affair. We'd walk up the street near F and G Streets, NW and we went there on Halloween. We'd walk up and down F Street where people used to dress in costume much like they do in Georgetown these days, but this was on F Street. Sunday afternoons we'd go as a family. Shops weren't open in those days on Sundays. That was a later innovation.

(Joseph Eugene Zeis)

It was very interesting how we celebrated holidays in terms of family. As far as Fourth of July, we always went to my grandparents Blumenthal, down on Seventh Street. They had a store down on Seventh Street, NW between S and T. The sidewalk was very, very wide or so it seemed as a child, extremely wide. We would light

firecrackers and I could see all the people from the stores come out with their rocking chairs and they would watch. We did the sparklers.

(Flora Blumenthal Atkin)

The major Jewish holidays were both in the fall. One was the serious day of atonement and the other was the Sukkot, which was the festival of harvest. The first one is serious and the second is a more fun holiday. Well, the first one we spent at my grandparents in Washington. It was a serious and sad one and somebody was always crying because they took the holiday seriously. Well, we went down there to stay because the synagogue was down at Sixth and I, and my parents wouldn't ride on the holiday, and so we would walk . . . I have very special

A White House Easter egg roll, c. 1943. (Courtesy Gallagher Collection, HSW Collections.)

memories of that block of Seventh Street and that house.

(Flora Blumenthal Atkin)

We went to the Easter Egg Roll every Easter at the White House. My grandmother took me and that was normal. That was Easter.

(Florence Crawford Marvil)

There was a Mrs. Peterson also who was a fascinating teacher who was full of love, kindness, and giving. If we didn't have proper clothes she would make sure we had something to wear. Mrs. Peterson had this stamp contest before Christmas. There was a vacant house right around the corner from school and this was the house of a doctor, someone who traveled. In the corner was a big bag of letters from all over the world. I took those letters to Mrs. Peterson and I got that prize. I kept that prize all wrapped up in a little box and I would shake it. I wasn't supposed to open it up until Christmas, so my mind just went all over. I did not know what it was. When I opened it up, it was a chocolate star for Christmas and I could hardly eat it, it was so hard. I was a little disappointed, because my imagination had carried me all around the world and back again.

(Loretta Carter Hanes)

Boys at 13 got Bar Mitzvahed. In Orthodox ceremonies men and women were segregated. You'd finish and then go up and kiss your mother and then go back down. We just had herring and a small snack and no big deal. Girls were not Bat Mitzvahed. My father taught other kids and me how to read the Torah for $1 a week. We also pursued our studies with Rabbi Klavan and his brother. I read the Chumash and the five books.

(Larry Rosen)

Charlie Brotman preparing for his Bar Mitzvah with his Talis covering his shoulders and his Siddu, in his hand, c. 1940. (Courtesy Charlie Brotman.)

I was Bar Mitzvahed and I celebrated Rosh Hashanah and Yom Kippur. I had my paternal grandparents on Georgia Avenue and Otis Place, NW who had a meat market, though it was not a kosher butcher and I had my maternal grandparents in Baltimore . . . We used to celebrate various holidays in

55

Damon Cordom standing proudly with his parents in front of their Christmas tree, 1935. (Courtesy Damon Cordom.)

both places. My mother's father was the tailor for the czar in Russia and on Passover, and especially Chanukah, my grandfather used to sew little cloth bags and however old you were, you got that many pennies in the bag. It was the days when penny money was great. They couldn't afford more, but it was great.

(Charles Brotman)

Christmas was sparse in my family, and in a number of families as well. We had no live Christmas tree. My mother had a stick of a tree that you would put on a tabletop. You would fan out the three or four little limbs that you had and you would throw bulbs on it and an awful lot of tinsel on it and you would celebrate Christmas. I usually went to Bill and Curly Patten's house for a live tree or my aunt and uncle had one. The

thing that was enjoyable was the hanging stocking. Because I liked nuts, my parents would stuff it with pecans, walnuts, almonds, and tangerines—and oranges were hard to come by in the winter. If you could get one, that was a treat. There might be a coin in there. I liked raisins, so I would get a little bag of raisins thrown in. Those were the small gifts. You would hang the stockings from the bedposts, since there were no fireplaces.

(Damon Cordom)

There were so many different things that happened on U Street. We used to have Halloween parades and we used to go to the Boys Clubs on Thirteenth and U and watch movies. We participated in the Halloween procession when we were in grade school. We used to dress up but my brothers also had their birthdays around then so my mom would bake three cakes and we would have a big party.

(Lillie Latten)

I was always in the Christmas program. One time I was the angel and another time the narrator. A final year they wanted me to be the Virgin Mary and my mom put her foot down there. It was sort of a family joke that we would compromise so far and then no farther. I remember singing Christmas carols. I am sure it was a largely Christian school so we just fit in.

(Susan Tassler Ginsberg)

My father's birthday was Halloween and because of that, Halloween was a very special holiday. My mother made us costumes, and we went to a parade and went around Meridian Hill Park, and there was trick or treating in the apartment building.

(Susan Tassler Ginsberg)

Some holidays didn't amount to very much because of lack of income. My first Christmas in Washington, Santa forgot me. He didn't come until two weeks later, when I got a pair of skates. I remember all the excitement downstairs and my mother explained that Santa didn't come yet, but he would soon. After that we had better Christmases. We didn't have a lot of relatives that we celebrated with. I had two uncles, two aunts, and some cousins, but we didn't get together and do big family gatherings when I was young. It was the immediate family.

(James Davis)

We were sort of the more liberal newer Jewish. There were fewer Orthodox. We all went to Sunday school and were Bar Mitzvahed, but we hated it. We never got real serious. Passover was more fun; we made jokes and ran around like Indians instead of taking it seriously like we should have . . . We didn't go to services very much unless we had to or there was a special event. We did Chanukah. It was more exchanging gifts. We even exchanged gifts on Christmas—no Santa Claus or Christmas tree or anything like that.

(Sandy Berk)

We belonged to Washington Hebrew Congregation. I liked reading and getting to write. I didn't like sports too much. I was lousy at them. I had some good Spanish lessons. I remember doing a play in Spanish. I was the hand. I remember that we learned all the Christmas carols. It was before the school prayer decision so we would start every day with a prayer and there were a high percentage of kids who were Jewish, but that didn't seem to matter at the time, so we learned all the Christmas carols. I remember most of the lyrics, which I loved. It took quite a long time for my consciousness to be raised that we weren't supposed to be doing this.

(Alison Luchs)

Susan Tassler (back row) and Alan Tassler preparing to trick or treat with friends on Park Road at Sixteenth and Harvard Streets, c. 1949. (Courtesy Susan Tassler Ginsberg.)

Rosh Hashanah, the New Year, Passover, Purim. I don't remember it emphasized as much in those days. We had a carnival at Purim and a Seder at Passover, which you celebrated at home. I don't remember if they said much in those days in the schools. Now they would be much more fair and if they discussed it at all they would bring in all the different holidays.

(Alison Luchs)

My cousins lived on McGill Terrace and we used to have big Thanksgiving dinners together with several branches—my mother's sister and her children and relatives on my father's side. There were some great Thanksgivings and Fourth of Julys when all these families with multiple kids would assemble, usually on McGill

Terrace. My two uncles had houses caddy-cornered on McGill Terrace and their backyards would sort of flow together with a big meadow between the two houses and we could have picnics and run around and play and that was really neat.

(Alison Luchs)

Christmas was big. One of our neighbors would dress up as Santa and come to our house on Christmas Eve. Sometimes, and this was more in our teen years, we would go down to Midnight Mass and we would take all the Protestants and Jewish and Catholic and everybody would walk down to St. Francis together for Midnight Mass. We brought the whole neighborhood down there and listened to that old lady sing "O Holy Night" and she could never get that

Children at a birthday party at the South African Legation, 1939. The two cowboys are (left) Jean-Louis Lucet, son of the third secretary of the French Embassy, and (right) Johnny Chramiec, the son of an Air and Military attache from Poland. (Courtesy the Patterson Collection, HSW Collections.)

high note. It was a great neighborhood . . . Christmas was my favorite holiday. Christmas Eve you'd get together and you'd eat a big meal and sometimes you'd go to Midnight Mass. Christmas Day you'd play with your new stuff, and one year, I think I was 15, and I got a skateboard. It was about 75 degrees that day and I got to go outside and use my new skateboard. Christmas was always wonderful. I'd get a new dress and you had new clothes and you had all the wonderful smells in the house. It was a big deal. But it was just family. It wasn't extended family for that . . . We didn't even have much family nearby.

(Judy Scott Feldman)

Fourth of July we went to the Washington Monument or we would watch with the neighbors three houses down and we had a gorgeous view. What really struck me was that back then you'd all go down after dinner and you'd all be standing around and then a firework would go off and you'd all go "ooh" and then you'd wait another four or five minutes. And then another firework would go off and you'd all go "aah" and the whole thing would last maybe an hour and you would see maybe 15 fireworks or so. When I went down this Fourth of July it was nonstop. It was great but totally different.

(Judy Scott Feldman)

The Fourth of July was a great cookout time. You could see the Capitol and the monuments from our house and so we didn't have to leave the house. We just took that for granted. So we would sit in the front and be like "ooh, wow" and we just took it for granted. We could see from our yard what people from all over the world want to see.

(Kim Jones)

Judy Scott Feldman and her sister Lisa decorating the family Christmas tree, 1960. (Courtesy Judy Scott Feldman.)

I remember Christmases before I was four years old. Everybody came over to my house. It was a big to do. Christmas was a kid's holiday, and in my family that meant that I had the great fortune of receiving the unbridled benefits of having tons of toys, hugs, and laughter around me. One particular Christmas, when I was four, I can clearly remember coming down the stairs and seeing a gigantic dollhouse, a train set, a doll, and a bicycle, and it was all for me. And, of course, there was breakfast. Christmas breakfast was the best! Coffee cake and grapefruit, surrounded by plates of bacon, scrambled eggs, biscuits, and grits. Yum!

(Tracy Ferguson)

I think my favorite holiday was Fourth of July and we'd go down to the Mall and make a big picnic and go with another family. Being out in the sun all day and being able to run around was pretty fantastic. There were 500,000 other people there. That's so cool. Everyone just comes and hangs out. Back then people could drink beer and bring big pieces of furniture onto the Mall. I think now security reasons make you stop that. I still do it now even without my family. It became not so cool to go with my family. It became clear to me that riding my bike down was the best way to get there. I would meet my friends . . . That was probably my favorite holiday in the city because it was a great excuse to be outside all day and the fireworks were great.

(Thaddeus Marcus Verhoff)

Kim Jones at a family picnic with brother Eugene, cousin Steven, cousin James, Aunt Ernestine, mother, and stepfather Claude Jackson, 1978. (Courtesy Kim Jones.)

3. CONNECTING THE LOCAL WITH THE NATIONAL

I remember the 1919 riot, and I can remember looking out my window on Twelfth and U, and I can remember the commotion and being frightened. I remember it was July. I heard them talking about the riot when girls working at the Bureau were afraid to come home and the fellas went to see that they got home okay. My parents kept me inside.

(Helen Combs Wood)

I remember World War I. I was nine years old in 1917. There were military personnel on the streets, posters all around, and lots of people selling war bonds. They gave speeches and put barrels on the street into which you were supposed to deposit peach and prune pits to be used to combat the use of gas. They went into gas masks. It was just remarkable to see that sort of thing going on. A sign said, "Win the war. Deposit pits here." Airplanes were not common, but once in awhile a plane would fly over the city and it would discharge pamphlets to the city. "Buy War Bonds." There were lots of military personnel around the city.

(Frank R. Jackson)

I remember the Great Depression. My father fortunately continued to work. Probably the Bonus Marchers stand out as much as anything during that period. I was in the Scouts at that time and we used to cross the Mall area going from my house to Third and C Streets where the group met. We'd pass through where the Bonus Marchers were all on the Mall. The Bonus Marchers were well-behaved and well-intentioned people. They set up these shelters and some of them went through great deals of pain to decorate them and make them look like homesteaders. They had decorated them with stones, walkways, flags, and other things. They were all over the Mall in their house settings.

(Joseph Eugene Zeis)

We also had an interesting experience on Easter Monday and the rule was that no adult could go to the grounds of the White House for the Easter Egg Roll without a child. So we would hang around the West Gate and when we would see an adult being turned away, we would sneak up and offer to hold that person's hand while we

Bonus Army camps on Third and Pennsylvania Avenue, NW, 1932. (Courtesy HSW Collections, CHS 8000A.)

hid our face and walked in. Then we would scurry over to the East Gate and walk out and run around and wait for another customer. The police down there knew our racket. We charged whatever coin was in that person's hand—usually a nickel and sometimes a dime, but a nickel was pretty good back in 1922 or '23. Those were the good old days.

(Markus Ring)

There were three other kids in the neighborhood and we used to go over to the White House about once a week to exercise President Harding's dog, a champion Airedale by the name of Laddie Boy. We met President Harding on four or five occasions and he would be standing in the door as we brought the dog back.

He would pat us on the head and send us back to the kitchen. Mr. Harding left orders that we were to be given ice cream, cookies, and milk in the White House kitchen after we walked the dog. We four fellas have voted Republican ever since.

(Markus Ring)

The Depression was an interesting phenomenon. Having a grocery store we had plenty to eat. There were a couple of chain stores around the same block, but our grocery store was the last one on the way to Bethesda. There was one in Rockville and one in Georgetown, but ours delivered. We had a pretty good-sized delivery business and Montgomery County was not too well developed.

(Marvin Tievsky)

There are some events that are peculiar to Washington. Inaugural parades are certainly among them. My first inaugural was Calvin Coolidge's on March 4, 1925. What made it unusual was the perch from which I watched: the steel girder that held up the sign for Keith's Theater. Keith's, the vaudeville house on Fifteenth Street across from the Treasury, was where Woodrow Wilson had loved to watch stage acts while he was president. It was convenient for him, being one block from the White House. And it was convenient for me, since the sign hung right outside my father's office on the second floor of the Albee Building . . . The parade was especially memorable for the sight of those World War I tanks rumbling up Fifteenth Street, making their screeching turns on the streetcar tracks.

(Austin Kiplinger)

Another prerequisite of growing up in Washington is the opportunity to meet big names in the news. For me, the first such big name was Herbert Hoover, whose campaign headquarters in 1928 were in the Barr Building on Seventeenth Street overlooking Farragut Square. When my father asked if I would like to bring a friend down some Saturday morning to meet the candidate, my buddy Woody Saugstad and I were breathless with excitement. We were ushered into the candidate's presence; he spoke some pleasantries, and shook our hands. As we left, Woody and I said to each other, incredulous, "We just shook hands with a man who may be president of the United States!" And so we had.

(Austin Kiplinger)

In 1932, my father had taken me down to Pennsylvania Avenue to see the Bonus Army—veterans of World War I who were

Markus Ring outside his father's store on Seventeenth Street, NW, 1921. (Courtesy Markus Ring.)

Bonus Army camps in Anacostia, 1932. (Courtesy HSW Collections, CHS 5440.)

encamped in dilapidated old buildings along the avenue where the Federal Triangle now stands. Because of the Depression, they had come to ask Congress for early payment of a veterans' bonus scheduled for 1945. We walked among the marchers, then crossed the Eastern Branch to see others in their makeshift shelters—tin huts in the mud of the Anacostia Flats.

(Austin Kiplinger)

We were affected by the Depression. My father was selling securities in 1929 and everything we had was invested, including my college money. Our house was almost taken away, but the homeowner's loan came and let you refinance and lowered the payments. Somehow we managed to work it out. My relatives sent us food from their grocery stores because my father was out of work. Government employees often kept their jobs, but banks failed and people invested in the stock market lost their money, because it was bought on margin . . . Washington was not depression proof for everybody, but better for other people because of the government. People doing domestic work were out of work. It certainly affected us. It wasn't as bad as other cities. I don't remember bread lines. When the Bonus Marchers came they were pretty poor. That was a great day for us because we were able to buy a car with the bonus money. It was hard in Northwest because not that many people were affected by the Depression. Everybody wasn't so bad off. Some of them worked for the government and they still had their jobs. We worried about losing the house. We'd open a can of fruit and have it for two nights. It was a struggle. I would wear my cousin's clothes.

(Janet Kasdon Lobred)

Back then when you dated, it was very acceptable to go to the hotels to dance. Hotels would never serve us liquor, but they were too willing to serve Cokes. On Sundays they had tea dances. The Roosevelt Hotel, a block down from where I lived, was run by Maria Kramer of New York, and she introduced the big bands from New York to Washington and Glenn Miller opened the tea dance at the Roosevelt Hotel—and I was there. I was at the Roosevelt tea dance on Pearl Harbor day . . . We didn't even know where Pearl Harbor was, but we got into our date's car and we drove over to the Japanese Embassy and we watched the smoke go up when they were burning all of their credentials. They were at war with us now, so they were burning their files.

(Florence Crawford Marvil)

World War II arrived when I was a junior in high school. Gasoline was the first commodity to be rationed. High school cafeterias were used for the public to fill out the necessary forms and students volunteered to help as sort of policemen to shepherd the public to seats, one of us patrolling the aisles and signaling to another at the door that a seat was available for the next person. Another wartime change in our routine was a change in school hours. Instead of 9 to 3, they were now 9:30 to 3:30. Since Washington did not run school buses, those of us living too far to walk had to take public transportation, and so many workers were crowding into the city, this change of hours eased a little of the crush.

(Jo Forbes Carpenter)

During the Depression Mrs. Roosevelt had a clothing and food program. As a child I would stand outside the lunchroom and the woman there said, "No, little girl. Go home." I said I was hungry, and Mrs. Roosevelt walked up and she lifted me up and said, "If this little girl ever comes to this door asking for food . . . " After that I had no problem. Mrs. Roosevelt helped me. And that's why she was in my heart for the March of Dimes.

(Loretta Carter Hanes)

I remember the day war was declared. My mother and I were on the bus going to my grandmother's. A little boy was out with the newspapers and had to tell the major events of the day to sell the papers. It didn't affect me so much. My father didn't go to war. There was only one person close to me

Jo Forbes Carpenter on the back steps of her Fessenden Street bungalow, 1941. (Courtesy Jo Forbes Carpenter.)

65

who went. I knew it was going on, but it really didn't touch me much. It didn't change anything or affect us except for rations—the short little red button we used to get sugar from the store. We were limited in shoes. Nylons were limited. We had to stand in line. We had books/tokens and we had this little red button, I think for

sugar. It did affect us now that I think about it. In that regard it was always in your mind that war was going on, but that was about it.

(Mary Meade Coates)

World War II was an exciting time. We became aware that something was going on

Walkie talkie demonstrations at the Back the Attack War Show on the Mall, 1943. (Courtesy Goode WW II Collection, HSW Collections.)

World War II preparations included blackout curtains, 1943. (Courtesy Goode WWII Collection, HSW Collections.)

because there seemed to be more people around, particularly the military. One thing that none of my friends did, but I took quite an interest in, were military patches and regimental pins. I developed a little spiel and would approach the military men, both enlisted and officers, to ask them if they had any spare chevrons, regimental pins, or other types of military insignia. Over time I was able to collect a couple of cigar boxes worth of these things.

(Damon Cordom)

On December 7, 1941 I was eight years old and my dad and I were listening to the Redskins game on the radio, and they came on with an announcement that the Japanese had bombed Pearl Harbor. There was a lot of commotion in the neighborhood and neighbors came out on the street and everyone was talking. Probably by about 4:30 in the afternoon there was an Extra out about it. You know, "Extra, Extra! Read all about it!" We had blackout drills where we had to pull the blinds and the wardens would come around. I remember rationing came in not long after that. I was quite a rough and tumble little boy and so I wore shoes out pretty quickly. Well, shoes were rationed, but my dad had a couple of brothers who were married, but didn't have any children, so he would always collect coupons from them so they could get me a pair of shoes.

Timothy Burton attended Gonzaga High School on I and North Capitol Streets, NW. (Courtesy Wymer Photo Collection, HSW Collections.)

My dad would always say a pair of shoes for me lasted about a month. They'd be new, two weeks later they'd go into the repair shop, and then two weeks after they were worn out. I played a lot of marbles and wore out the toes.

(Tom Reese)

My father was excited about Harry Truman and I remember thinking he was my childhood president. My father took me to the inaugural parade but due to weather we watched it from a bar on television. When he left town we went to the hotel on Sixteenth Street where he was staying and then to Union Station to wave him back to Missouri.

(Susan Tassler Ginsberg)

I was taken by my father to the National Press Club. I was about six and it was some father-daughter event. I remember being bored with the speeches and playing with the sugar bowl and my father telling me not to fidget. Truman and Margaret were there and they played the Missouri Waltz, a duet. Another time when I was in high school or college and Eleanor Roosevelt was going to speak, my father asked me to go and I was in a bad mood so I said I didn't want to go. I have always regretted that. I should have just gotten over my bad mood.

(Susan Tassler Ginsberg)

Air raid drills. We would go out into the hall and curl up into the fetal position and duck our heads with our hands up over our head. I found it sort of exciting. I don't think I comprehended how horrible it would be if something really happened. It was exciting and out of the ordinary.

(Alison Luchs)

In seventh grade I remember John F. Kennedy's assassination. The principal put the announcement over the loud speaker so everybody heard the announcement. Of course, with John F. Kennedy being the first Catholic president, the Sisters were bedazzled by him. They were almost like little John F. Kennedy groupies or something. But, of course, when the announcement came across, Sister Elizabeth just started weeping and wailing in the classroom very openly. Everything seemed bright and promising and this seemed to come out of nowhere. It was a disturbing experience because you just don't expect the president to get shot.

(Timothy Burton)

The riots of 1968. I was a junior at Gonzaga. We had gone in the morning in our carpool. Martin Luther King Jr. had been assassinated the day before and city officials and school officials let us out about 1 o'clock for our safety. Unfortunately this was one of the days that the guy who was driving the car for the carpool had left early and my brother and I had to fend for ourselves. This usually wasn't a problem because there was a bus on M Street that we could catch that went all the way to New Carrollton. It was just three blocks away. We would catch the bus every once and a while. We went up to catch the bus and just as we got there, the bus started to pull away and we banged on the door and the bus driver didn't hear us or ignored us and we were left standing alone at the bus stop on North Capitol Street. It wasn't really a bad

neighborhood and there weren't really a lot of houses around there. We weren't in the middle of Shaw or anything. There was a junior high school about two and a half blocks away on M Street, and they were let out for safety too. All the kids came pouring out down M Street. It was an all-black school, and my brother and I were the only two white people at the bus stop. My brother said, "What do you want to do?" And I said, "Well we haven't done anything so we should just stay here and wait for the bus." I wasn't really expecting anything. Well, they got closer and this one girl hits me square in the face. I wasn't really expecting this and it was humiliating also. It hurt my pride. And so all of the sudden some other girl from the crowd goes, "Leave them alone. They didn't do anything." That was the end of it, but we ended up going back to the high school and ended up getting a ride with somebody's mother who was going up the Southwest freeway to PG County and said that she would drop us off. So that's my riot story.

(Timothy Burton)

I was in school when John F. Kennedy was shot. I was in a Catholic school, so of course our principal came on the school public address system and she said that the president had been shot. I remember that we all got down beside our desks and we prayed. We loved him a great deal. They sent us home and my mother came and got us and when we got home my great aunt was on her knees before the television set and prayed for him because the television wasn't telling us what had happened. We were heartbroken. Everybody was heartbroken. He was so young and we felt so optimistic about him. We felt he was doing so much for us and that we were included in the country, so there was a feeling of great optimism. That was a horrible, horrible day.

(Breena Clarke Cooper)

[I was] at Thirteenth and Clifton living with an aunt of mine at my cousin's house. I was around five or six. I remember a lot of city unrest. I remember riots and I remember the day MLK was shot. My parents had told me a few things about Dr. King. I didn't remember much and knew he did good things. I remember the day he was shot and for some time after that when I would be sitting in the car or sitting down and anytime a white person walked by I would hide behind the car or crouch because I took the events of the day to mean white people kill blacks. For a few months or so I was scared and, of course, my parents straightened me out . . . I witnessed the riot and had family members who were beaten and tear gassed. It was nothing like the riots in Mount Pleasant we had a while back. I was so amazed with the way things have changed and the restraint of the police, the way they just sat back and allowed themselves to get bombarded in Mount Pleasant. With the 1968 riots their riot sticks were a lot bigger and they were using them a lot more and there was a lot more tear gas and violence. It looked like something you would see on the evening news that was far away. It was right around Thirteenth, Clifton, and Euclid, in that area. It made me aware of things and was eye opening . . . With the riots my parents wouldn't allow me to go outside, but I could see all the mayhem and violence. At one point my family members came in the door choking and crying tears and all that because they were outside. The riots really weren't talked about. They talked about injustices and when people are oppressed

this is what happens. They didn't teach me hating white people or anything like this. They explained to me certain facts like somebody killed Martin Luther King, people were upset, there was poverty and injustice, and this is what happens when people are upset.

(Desmond Leary)

The thing I really remember about junior high school was the bus was taking a detour home and something had happened on Connecticut Avenue to Ronald Reagan and the first reports of the assassination attempt was that some secret serviceman had got shot and that was it. I remember being in sixth period and knowing something happened on Connecticut Avenue at the hotel, but that was all it was. And then I got home and I find out that the president was shot and I just remembered being detoured around the hospital because everyday the bus ride home went by the hospital where Reagan was, that they eventually named after him.

(Keith Lofton)

I was about three and a half and it was Carter's inauguration. My father's office overlooked Pennsylvania Avenue. I watched from his office window. It was on the 1400 block. The office isn't even there anymore, but it was on the east side of the White House. I had no idea what was going on. I remember four years later and I was rooting for Ronald Reagan and they asked why and I said because I wanted there to be another parade. They said there would be another parade no matter what.

(Adam Vann)

I remember Ronald Reagan being elected president. I remember my mother asking me who I would vote for in the election. It must have been around 1979, and I answered Ronald Reagan and my parents were staunch Democrats and were just so shocked. "Why would you do that?" "Well,

he hasn't had a term yet." Well, sharing was a big thing when you were little kids.

(Thaddeus Marcus Verhoff)

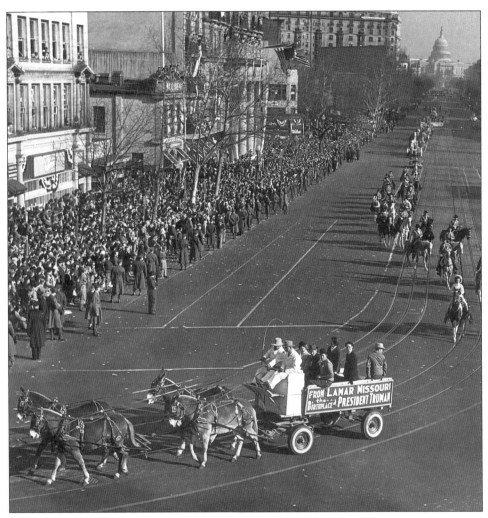

Inaugural parade of President Truman, 1949. (Courtesy HSW Collections, CHS 06622.)

4. LEARNING IN SCHOOL AND BEYOND

Garnet-Patterson Junior High. There was a red brick building with eight rooms named Garnet and back behind it was another red brick eight-roomed building named Patterson. That's why when the junior high school was made, they named it Garnet-Patterson Junior High . . . We left school at 12 and came home for lunch. School was at Twelfth and U and we walked home for lunch. After school we just came home and most of the parents were home. There was always someone home.

(Helen Combs Wood)

Dr. Drew was in my class. He sat behind me in class. He was in the same year in high school with me. He was in the club I was in. They had parties and we would go together. Charlie Drew sat right behind me in math class. At that time bobbed hair was just beginning to get popular and my mother cut mine and he used to play with my hair.

(Helen Combs Wood)

The Carnegie Library. We had little library cards and we went there regularly. We took the streetcar and probably we walked. We went with friends because we were old enough to go by ourselves. We would go regularly. You could keep books two weeks and if books were late you had to pay 2¢ or something. It was public so we could go. I didn't pay attention if there were other children there. It was a cardboard colored card. Teachers would give us assignments to do there.

(Helen Combs Wood)

I used to go to the library a lot at Seventh Street and New York Avenue, NW, the Carnegie Library. Strangely that was not segregated. I read everything, but *Gulliver's Travels, Robinson Crusoe,* and the *King Arthur* series were my favorites.

(Frank R. Jackson)

I went to Bruce School on Kenyon Street for elementary school and Dunbar for high school. Dunbar was a wonderful school. We thought it was the best high school in the city. There were only two black high schools in the city at the time. Dunbar was an outgrowth of the old M Street High School, and the faculty and teachers were just marvelous. There were so many of them who were scholars. I entered in 1921.

(Frank R. Jackson)

Lifeguards Joseph Drew, Charles Drew, and an unidentified friend at the Francis Pool, c. 1930. (Courtesy Grace Ridgeley Drew.)

The educational facilities were segregated and we walked from Fifteenth and T Streets to Seventeenth and M Streets, NW to attend Sumner School. Most of us had to walk distances in order to get to the colored schools, as they called them then. Sumner, of course, is still in existence but not as a school, as a museum. First of all they had a front door, but you didn't use that entrance, that was reserved for dignitaries. There were side entrances and you went in the side entrances. I remember very distinctly the first day that I was enrolled there, my mother took me and of course we went through the front door. When I went by myself when the school actually opened, I didn't know any better. Those sacred steps were reserved for the dignitaries. I was met at the door by one of the teachers and she had to send me back out to the playground to get in line with the other children to come in that side door. I enjoyed myself at Sumner. They had very good teachers. At Sumner the grades would range from kindergarten to eighth grade. We used to go across the street to take sewing classes. When you left the eighth grade, you always wore a midi blouse and skirt for graduation, and we had to make our midi blouse and skirt for graduation.

(Marion Jackson Pryde)

I went to Dunbar High School and then Miner College. I got a position in public schools when I was 19 after finishing Miner

[Teacher's College]. We were at an advantage because we had excellent teachers who were trained at Smith and other great colleges like Howard and Radcliffe. Dr. Simpson studied at the Sorbonne and couldn't get positions in white places. We had first-class teachers. We loved the Dramatic Club because Miss Burrill was in charge. We'd either participate in the play or backstage. We put on *Bluebird* over at Armstrong and it was quite a production. In one scene the bluebirds flashed across the screen and she wanted some noise like the bluebirds were singing. There was a little whistle you could buy and dip into water to make a little birdlike sound. I remember going down to the 10¢ store with another girl to get these whistles. We were dipping whistles into

buckets of water behind the screens, blowing whistles, and spilling water.

(Marion Jackson Pryde)

I went to Business High. Central was where all the kids were going. That was the upscale school. My father always wanted me to be a lawyer and he didn't have any college education, but he was doing all right. I didn't know a lawyer from one to another. I knew it had something to do with business so my father said well if you don't want to be a lawyer at least go into business, so he wanted me to go to Business High. I learned shorthand, typing, bookkeeping. So that's where I went . . . I got to Business High when I was 12 years old. I'll never forget, I got into the classroom and all of the teachers were

Going to a space free from racial barriers, such as the Old Central Library, popularly called the Carnegie Library, was a rare and pleasurable experience in segregated Washington. (Courtesy HSW Collections, CHS 09120.)

Dunbar High School, the premier high school for African-American students in Washington. (Courtesy Wymer Photo Collection, HSW Collections.)

just so wonderful. They were just so nice and one of the teachers was a mathematics teacher and her name was Florence Judge. She was single and lived on Columbia Road in a high-class apartment on Mount Pleasant Street and Columbia Road. Helen White taught in geography. I became a high school cadet. My mother thought I shouldn't do that. She didn't like the idea of her son being a soldier, because they were the first ones to go if we went to war. My father was a little different and he said let him be there. My grades were good. I was always doing my homework. I was a buck private my first year and a corporal my second year and top sergeant my third year. I carried a sword. I was 15 or 16 when I was a captain. Can you imagine? I was just a kid!

(Robert Israel Silverman)

We had a competition to see who would get the scholarship to George Washington University. Best all around and not just academic. I happened to be captain of the winning company and I had just about all As, so I got the scholarship. I had good grades, the debating team, the high school band, and everything. The scholarship was between me and Ida Bush. The story I got later on in life is that she withdrew her name because she thought that I would have had it because I was captain of the winning Cadet Company. So I paid no tuition for four years.

(Robert Israel Silverman)

I went to elementary school on Tenth and E Streets, SW, the Fairbrother School. It was half a block from where we lived. Junior High was on Sixth and Virginia Avenue, SW,

75

Jefferson Junior High and McKinley Technical High School was on Second and T Streets, NE. I went there the first year the building opened in 1928. I went to Jefferson Junior High and graduated in 1928. They had a seventh, eighth, and ninth grade so I started in 1925. There was a great deal of pride in that new school. I wasn't involved in athletics, but they practically swept the city in athletics—football, track, and the cadets. It was just a marvelous school with all kinds of opportunities there. They had a number of shops there— wood shop, electric shop, print shop, and other fascinating places. Tech was a beautiful school with a lot of facilities there. Well, I studied printing. I'd intended to be a printer. I heard about an apprentice printer at the government printing office and with

that in mind I followed printing through Junior High and High school, and when I got out of school printers were walking the streets. In 1931 these were tough times and I filed an application with the Printing Office, but people were walking the streets so they surely didn't need apprentices. I didn't get a call until about 1938 or 1939. By that time I had joined the fire department.

(Joseph Eugene Zeis)

In the fall of 1930, I enrolled in McKinley Technical High School in Washington, D.C. By this time I was 5'10" and weighed 155 pounds. My friend, Kemp Smith, and I thought we might go out for the football team. However, when we lined up on the field along with about 50 other boys, the coach came down the line, shoved me, and

Joseph Eugene Zeis standing in Southwest, c. 1929. (Courtesy Joseph Eugene Zeis.)

Cadet Corps Lt. Col. Markus Ring standing at attention, 1935. (Courtesy Markus Ring.)

said, "Join the Cadets, boy. You'll get hurt here." This gives you some idea of the size of the other fellows. I joined the High School Cadet Corps. I ended up, by my senior year, a first lieutenant of Company C of the First Battalion, Second Regiment. We had a marvelous regiment and a marvelous time.

(Markus Ring)

Washington high schools in those years were still segregated, with five for white children [Western, Central, Eastern, Tech, and Business] and two for African Americans [Dunbar and Armstrong] . . . As a matter of fact, all the schools were remarkably good then. Dunbar, with its large percentage of faculty members with Ph.D.s, catered to promising students from educated families, many of whom came from other cities especially for a Dunbar education.

(Austin Kiplinger)

I spent grades four through eight in the Janney School. There was no middle school or high school in Tenleytown. We went to Western High School in Georgetown, which is now the Duke Ellington School. Janney was a fine school with very fine teachers. I liked just about everything. It was a brand new school at the time. There was a playground in the back, though not as big as it is now. There were woods in the back and we used to play back there. Western was the best high school in the city in those days. We had children of diplomats and the officers' children from Fort Myers in Virginia. I was 11 years old when I entered high school and 15 when I graduated. I skipped many grades. I went on to college and was tending my dad's grocery store. At GW [George Washington University] I studied

Flora Blumenthal Atkin in costume for the Hoffman and Hoskins May ball, c. 1925. (Courtesy Flora Blumenthal Atkin.)

business and accounting. When I graduated it was tough, because it was in the middle of the Depression.

(Marvin Tievsky)

I started dancing lessons probably at age three. From the very beginning I was interested in it. My parents took us to the Garden Pier in Atlantic City and they had dancing. I saw the dancing on the stage and I went out in the aisle and danced immediately. I would dance and sing at the drop of a hat. My first dancing lessons were the Isadora Duncan type of dance for the first year. After that I went to Hoffman and Hoskins, which was very, very well known in Washington. It was the place to go. I was one of a group of seven year olds, there were six of us, who were considered her stars. We always got the lead parts in the recitals and the May Balls. The May Balls were the big shows in May and they were held at either the National Theater or the Belasco Theater or the Gaeity Theater or any of the big theaters for two nights [Friday and Saturday nights]. I was very good except there was a special thing you had to do with acrobatics and I was not a daredevil by any means. You had to do a chest roll and I was scared to death to do it. You get down on your knees and you tuck your head all the way into your toes and you roll

over and land on your feet. But I was very determined.

(Flora Blumenthal Atkin)

I chose Roosevelt because it was a brand new school. I was in the first graduating class that went all the way through. Roosevelt became an academic and a business school. I was in the Spanish Club and the Keyboard Club and in the school operettas and the Math Club. I was in all these things and president of some of them . . . I was two years ahead of school for my age. That was the style back then. If you were doing well they didn't enrich your program, they just shoved you ahead. So that by the time I was graduated from sixth grade, I should have been in fourth grade.

(Flora Blumenthal Atkin)

Florence Crawford Marvil's graduation from Central High School, 1942. (Courtesy Florence Crawford Marvil.)

The suburbs up until the 1950s had covenants not to sell to Greeks, Jews, Chinese, and whoever. You signed a covenant not to sell to these people. There was a secondary discrimination that existed. I was aware of this as a teenager. This is why I give so much credit to the teachers who wanted us to respect each other's background. I remember having Hungarian friends in school whose parents didn't speak English, but they did. My teachers asked them to come dressed in their Hungarian traditional clothes and to do the dances. So we learned what other people lived like and this is what was just wonderful really—at least in the school that I went to. At the time the D.C. schools were considered the best in the country. Dunbar was one of the best schools in the United States . . . The D.C. public schools were great. We all spoke English—one language. It was a segregated community. There's no denying that. But it was a safe community.

(Florence Crawford Marvil)

Loretta Carter Hanes attended Shaw Junior High School in the 1930s. (Courtesy Wymer Photo Collection, HSW Collections.)

We lived at 2461 P Street and then 1272 Twenty-fifth Street. I attended Phillips Elementary School, which is now the International School on M Street between Twenty-seventh and Twenty-eighth Streets, Francis Junior High, and then Dunbar High School, Class of 1943. I went there because I wanted to go to college. We walked to Dunbar sometimes. We walked all over Washington. Connie Stokes lived at 2453 P Street and I lived at 1272 Twenty-fifth Street and we'd meet at Twentieth and P Streets. We'd walk to Eighteenth Street and Florida Avenue and pick up another little lady and go around the corner to U Street and then pick up Laverne Hall and walk to Dunbar. We thought nothing of it. Later on we started getting school tickets for 3¢ and ride the bus from Twenty-second and P Streets and ride to Third and P Streets, NW and then walk to school. We walked

everywhere. On Sunday afternoon we called having an enjoyable time going to church and then my friend Colleen Thompson and I would take our little patent leather shoes and walk to the Lincoln Memorial, the monuments, and the Capitol and walk back. Nobody had transportation or cars.

(Clara Sharon Taylor)

The teachers made the difference. They had gone to school and they gave you their knowledge. We concentrated on black history. Every day was black history. You didn't just do it once a day or once a month, everyday. You learned your songs. You learned about your heroes. All these people came in person like Mary McLeod Bethune. They came in person to inspire you. You read about Frederick Douglass every day; it wasn't every once and awhile.

*Mary Meade Coates attended Randall Junior High School on First and I Streets, SW.
(Courtesy Wymer Photo Collection, HSW Collections.)*

And therefore this empowered you to be more like Frederick Douglass, just like my mom grew up like Douglass. Everything was segregated. I was in intermediate grades when Bethune came, maybe fifth grade. They all embraced you and loved you and inspired you to do your best and your very best. That's why it was so unusual to see people failing. They have everything and we had nothing, but we had people to inspire us and they taught us how to struggle. We were taught whatever you do, don't be ashamed of the job that you do. Now if you aren't in the white shirt with the briefcase you are embarrassed. We used to respect that. There was pride for the dressmaker and barber and street cleaner. We did a lot of poetry. Paul Dunbar was one of my favorites.

(Loretta Carter Hanes)

Mrs. Harriet Boxdale Short, who worked at Howard, walked passed my house and I would sit on my steps and throw stones at her. She was beautiful and I just wanted her attention. So one day she said, "Look girl, what is your name?" I told her and she said, "I want to speak with your mother." I got so scared, but I got my mother and Harriet said, "Mrs. Carter I want to teach Loretta how to tap." My mother said fine. She'd take me to her little sorority room at Howard and I ended up dancing for a March of Dimes benefit. I did this while others would sleep, because this was a midnight show. So every evening I would get home from school, go to sleep, and rest. Then the neighbors would walk me to Redeemers Hall for rehearsal at Twelfth Street. We'd practice. "While Others Sleep" was the name of the show. My whole community would take me to rehearse. This was Delta Sigma Theta.

(Loretta Carter Hanes)

[I remember] going to school and coming home to eat lunch—Syphax School at Half and N Street, SW. Mrs. Locke was my second grade teacher. School was right near home, just a few blocks away across M Street. I went through fifth grade at Syphax and then transferred to Bowen, because Syphax was overcrowded. I went there in sixth grade and then I graduated.

(Mary Meade Coates)

We had a teacher that had us diagramming sentences—that I loved. For some reason I really loved that. He was a dynamite teacher. We had some good teachers that were almost like your parents too. They were truly dedicated. That is a difference from now. Now people say kids can't learn and that has to do with the teacher. During that time the teacher may live right next door to you because we were limited to where we could live, regardless of what you did. There were built in baby-sitters if a mother worked. At the time I wanted them to mind their own business, but now I truly appreciate it. Everyone would tell you to go home if they saw you someplace you weren't supposed to be. We really cared about each other back then. We had to. We were all there was.

(Mary Meade Coates)

Richard Mansfield and rows of kids waving to the camera from the War Bond drive at the Atlas Theater, 1941. (Courtesy Richard Mansfield Collection, HSW Collections.)

I was at Weightman for first and second grade. I was treated differently for those years, because my first language was Greek. I didn't speak English and I had a hard time understanding the teacher. When I heard my name, I would stand up and be mute. My teacher found this quite annoying, understandably so. She would pin notes to my sweater and I would take them home. The note, in effect, said, "Mr. Cordom you have to teach your child English. He doesn't understand class lessons." My dad would march me up the next morning and tell her, "My job is not to teach my son English. That's your job." I remember bringing those notes home every few days and, little by little, I was just forced to learn English, because I got immersed.

(Damon Cordom)

I remember bond drives. At the grammar school every Thursday we had a sale of savings stamps. You could buy stamps for as little as a quarter and you would buy your stamps and when you got enough stamps to fill a book up to $18.75 you could turn those in for a savings bond. They used to keep a record of how much in savings stamps were purchased by the kids in the school and when it got to a certain level, kids in the school could pick a piece of equipment for the war. The sixth graders

A model store in Park View Elementary School teaching children how to use war ration books, c. 1943. (Courtesy of Goode WWII Collection, HSW Collections.)

got to choose and we chose a half-track. They actually brought one up and put it on the playground so we could see it—this piece of equipment that we had helped pay for. That was actually a big, exciting moment for us.

(Tom Reese)

When you went to school, you had stamps to buy for a penny. If you filled your book with stamps—$10 books or $5 if I am not mistaken—if you filled the book, the big tanks would give you a ride down the steps on V Street. [We] had books when food was rationed and you had to cut out the stamp—almost like a food stamp, but these were smaller. There were different stamps for different food groups. A penny went a long way back then because you could get two pieces of candy for a penny or a big candy cane.

(Lillie Latten)

We didn't have varsity sports and just played different teams inside the school itself. I went to Cardozo High School. Central got turned over to the colored in 1950. My sister went and graduated in 1953 as the first class. I think that was the first school that the whites had that they turned over to the colored. That school had everything in there. We had drill teams. We had football teams. We had basketball teams. We had track teams. My brother ran track for Cardozo. He had trophies, all kinds of trophies. Everyone knew him.

(Lillie Latten)

I used to like all the musical movies because I took dancing lessons down at the Y, the YWCA. I took tap dancing, after that I took toe dancing and ballet, and then we had recitals over at different stadiums where they had the football teams. We had

a recital over there and then the dance teacher moved her studio over there on U Street. Her name was Doris Patterson over there on U Street.

(Lillie Latten)

In school we had 5¢ for a whole week and we could get a bottle of milk and two graham crackers. They used to have a bottle of milk with the cream on top. Oh god, that was some good milk. That was really milk then. That was in elementary school. A penny a day for milk and graham crackers, too. I just loved the milk and the cream.

(Lillie Latten)

Harvard Hall had a swimming pool downstairs and I remember my mother doing the sidestroke and my father doing a stroke he made up and looked like a walrus splashing around. My parents taught me, but when I was in high school I had a friend who was getting certified and she taught me in a class with other people. I learned to dive and swim in ten feet of water. I was very advanced then. We went swimming in Meridian Hill Apartments in a big pool.

(Susan Tassler Ginsberg)

I was a patrol boy at Kelly Miller Junior High at Forty-ninth and Brooks Street, NE. I rose from being a private to a captain from fourth to sixth grade. We would actually stop traffic like police officers. We thought we were police officers and we would assist children crossing the street. On the heavy traffic streets there were two of us on either side of the street stopping traffic, so that worked well. It also gave us a close kinship with the school police officer, because every school actually had a patrol police officer assigned to them. Sometimes the

Girls learning to dance at the Lucille Banks Dance School, 1300 block of U Street, NW. (Courtesy Robert H. McNeill.)

police officer would work the corners with us.

(James Davis)

At Spingarn I remember mostly the coaches because I had a lot of experiences with the coaches. The basketball coach was Mr. William Roundtree and another coach was Dave Brown. I played basketball and was on the track team. I was a high jumper. Dave Brown was in charge of football, track, and health and hygiene. He was quite a teacher and a motivator of young men. That's why I remember him and Mr. Roundtree so well. They were men you could admire and respect with a lot of integrity.

(James Davis)

In high school I remember going down to Congress and lobbying for home rule. My mother's kind of activism wasn't as much political as getting things done. She lobbied for the Chevy Chase Community Center, which was nice when they got the new building. I took ceramic lessons there when I was ten. They had all kinds of lessons and programs. It was a great community center.

(Alison Luchs)

We had lessons in piano. The Conservatory is still on T. My oldest cousin's relatives began that conservatory at the turn of the century. The Washington Conservatory of Music. We took lessons from one of the aunts . . . We were there for almost ten years from 4 to 14. We would get there on the bus. My parents and aunts and uncles came to watch us play. We always had a piano in the house. My mother had aspirations of going to Oberlin for music school. There was a musical tradition in the home. My grandmother sang while my mother played.

(Gretchen Roberts-Shorter)

I went to a debutante thing. We had to do a lot of practicing—dance, bowing, eating, etiquette, balance . . . It took a lot of work. Once a week for several months. My uncles were members so it was natural for us to belong. The club was the Bachelor Benedict. It was a social, civic organization for African Americans. It was like a debutante cotillion. The activities are pretty much focused on the senior year in high school.

(Gretchen Roberts-Shorter)

I attended the elementary program with the Campus School from grades one through eight, which was a model school for CU [Catholic University] for teachers and psychologists. It was mostly doctors' and teachers' kids and some neighborhood kids. I got in because my older siblings attended. We had this wonderful thing at the Campus School called picnic day held at Turkey Thicket. We had relay races and scavenger hunts and a hot dog lunch. All of our activities were down at Turkey Thicket and they would walk us back to school for the afternoon.

(Mary Teresa Barrick Stilwell)

[Turkey Thicket] was kind of nifty. You could walk through the monastery gardens. There were lots of places to just go and collect yourself. I spent a lot of time at Turkey Thicket in high school. They had

Susan Tassler Ginsberg, father Bernard, and brother Alan in Meridian Hill Park, c. 1945. (Courtesy Susan Tassler Ginsberg.)

Breena Clarke, dressed up in white, practicing for her piano recital, 1958. (Courtesy Breena Clarke.)

one act play contests throughout the District and we went to different recreation centers. I loved the theater and the movies. I did a summer workshop at Catholic University. When my mother worked there she tried to get us into many things that would keep us out of trouble in the summer. This was a high school drama workshop. It was sort of run as a recruitment program for CU. Father Harkey was the director and I adored Father Harkey, so I was willing to go to this one. They took us to a Broadway show, *Oliver*, and that was fun. They took us up on the bus for the day.

(Mary Teresa Barrick Stilwell)

My brother and I took accordion lessons for about eight years. We started when I was in first grade. We moved to an interim location after Adelphi, right around the corner from William G. Nurseries. We took accordion lessons there. There was a door-to-door salesman, Mr. Ferrago, an old Hungarian man with a big mole in the middle of his forehead. He came with his assistant, a svelte, pretty young female. She said they offered music lessons, and my parents thought that was a good idea—that there should be some culture in the family somewhere. Not knowing what it entailed and being in the first grade we were like yeah, yeah. And he taught guitar, piano, or accordion. Of course, they brought the

Mary Teresa Barrick Stilwell's class at the Catholic University Campus School graduation on the Mullen Library Steps, 1962. (Courtesy Mary Teresa Barrick Stilwell.)

accordion to the house and you could actually see the instrument. You couldn't bring a piano. The accordion just seemed so sparkling. We probably should have chosen piano, but, of course, we chose accordion—and it wasn't from any strong tie to the accordion because it was a family tradition or anything. We just chose accordions and, of course, it probably wasn't the smartest instrument to have taken. It was the age when the guitars were going to blossom in rock music. Accordions were never going to blossom into rock music and accordions were just looked at as a nerdy instrument and you never really heard it much. Today it has a much more versatile place than when I was actually taking the lessons.

(Timothy Burton)

One of the games we played in school was little games like Miss Mary Mack where we would recite a poem and other dance games, which was my initial interest in the drill team, because it was part of dancing and choreographed marches. It was popular to be on the drill team. We twirled batons. It was fun and like our playground games. Competition was part of the parade. The performance during the parade was part of the competition, so we wanted to practice diligently to win the competition.

(Andrea Littlejohn)

I enjoyed the fact that my teacher let us do a lot of coloring and drawing in first grade and this helped us learn words. I enjoyed arts and crafts and reading and going to the school library but also going to Takoma Park Library on Second and Butternut Street, NW. I recall reading *Charlotte's Web*. I read a series of books about a boy named Henry. I loved words and I was in the

spelling bee in school. I represented my class in the school and came in second.

(Andrea Littlejohn)

Rabaut Junior High was in the neighborhood, and I went for seventh and eighth grades. I was studious and decided I wanted to go to private school so I could progress academically a little faster. The Hawthorne School operated by Eleanor and Sandy Orr at Seventeenth and M Streets, NW in the old Sumner School Building. I heard it was giving scholarships. The Sumner School was one of the oldest African-American schools in the District. When I went there, it was an alternative curriculum school. Basically Eleanor and Sandy were studying the effects of African Americans to learn math and science. It had kids from all backgrounds. The school offered scholarships in turn for the rights to use the findings. My parents had to pay tuition in later years. As a result of the research, Eleanor published a book called *Twice as Less*, published around 1984 or 1985. I haven't actually read it because the theoretical part is hard for me to digest. It was located next to the School Without Walls before it moved to the GW campus. I graduated the Hawthorne School as valedictorian and matriculated to Barnard.

(Andrea Littlejohn)

Going to the Hawthorne School was a big change, but I was already aware of the difference between Northwest and Northeast and even my neighborhood and west of Sixteenth. It wasn't a totally foreign atmosphere to me to go to Hawthorne. I took the E2 bus and the 54 . . . We didn't have school teams or competitions with other schools, because there were only about 50 people enrolled. We played spades card games during breaks. We did interact with School Without Walls because of its proximity. We didn't have a school prom. We had about three students graduating. We had three or four periods of classes a day and we took a break in the afternoon to the common room for any administrative stuff Headmaster Sandy would tell us. He taught history. We had math, art, history, Latin, Spanish, or French. We were tested and broken up into groups based on our ability. We had exams at the end of the year. It wasn't the regular type of curriculum where you learned certain things each semester. It was odd.

(Andrea Littlejohn)

I had started taking guitar lessons and I was into music. I was taking lessons at All Souls Church on Sixteenth and Harvard. I was growing up different from my peers and listening to different music. I had found WGTV on the radio, which is Georgetown University radio, which was real radical. They played rock 'n roll and heavy metal and experimental jazz and everything. It was like a lifesaver. By that time I was pretty different and people started to find out that I did different things. I remember casually asking what did you do last night and I said, "Oh, I saw Kiss" and that was in '76, and after that it was like oh, man, he is a warrior. After the seventh grade, I moved out to Columbia again with my father and I had a little suburban experience and I thought it was great.

(Desmond Leary)

The eleventh grade I got into the School Without Walls and that was when the fun started. Originally it was at Sixteenth and M, M on Sixteenth and Seventeenth and it was 1979. I go there and it's very interesting, lots of good classes, very unstructured. School Without Walls was a place for

people who didn't want to conform to the mainstream. If you found yourself not fitting in at other places then the School Without Walls was the place for you. There were still different groups: the homeboys, kids from Bolling Air Force Base, some kids richer than others, and some kids from Southeast. It wasn't one type of school against the other. It wasn't different groups against different groups. It was people who appreciated each other's differences and that was cool. I just thought, okay, this was a better mentality than normal, which is a big thing throughout my life. I have always been against the normal and School Without Walls is a good place for people like that. We still had to do work and we got report cards and things like that, but it was infinitely more interesting. The school moved to the campus of GW University. You know, we could take college courses. Going to class could be anywhere all over the city. When it was time for class, you'd just get on the bus and you'd go.

(Desmond Leary)

Francis Junior High in Northwest near Georgetown. After leaving elementary school, I went to a neighboring junior high and there were problems like no books, or the teachers were on strike, or we were running amuck, or perhaps I was getting on my parents' nerves, or some problem like that. My parents decided to put me in another school. This other school was just the opposite of what I came from already and it was some sort of international school full of a mixture of diplomats' kids, refugee kids, kids from up-and-coming Latin neighborhoods, and bused kids from a different situation. My family always took part in community and political activism and I'm sure my transplant was the doing of my parents in some way . . . The Francis

Richard Mansfield playing drums with members of a high school band, c. *1943. (Courtesy Richard Mansfield Collection, HSW Collections.)*

environment saved me from the environment that I was already in—only that it was a school that was a little more open-minded. It was a little ahead of the times in terms of involving all mixed classes and all mixed cultures in one setting. But, I mean, it has a historical presence in my family because my aunts went there and other older relatives.

(Keith Lofton)

We spent our days hanging out and having fun and even gossiping about what was going on in the neighborhood. But when I moved in with my grandmother, my environment was very different because my grandmother was very civically active so I was exposed to a lot of different things and a lot of different people. I didn't hang

around a lot because I didn't have a lot of time because me grandmother took me places with her and she stayed on me a lot about school. I would try to hang out with some of my friends because I was still in the same neighborhood and went to school with my old friends. But I had other stuff to do like keep my grades up and other responsibilities like cutting grass and cleaning up in my community, which started to become fun to me. When I first had to do it, those things didn't really appeal to me. But it showed me a sense of responsibility, a sense of myself. So I don't really have that many friends from Anacostia per se as I have friends who I met going to school. Some of my friends from high school I kept in touch with. It is so ironic because we have so many dreams

89

Emilie Crawford and friends clowning around the Portner Apartments, Fifteenth and U Streets, NW, c. 1930. (Courtesy of Florence Crawford Marvil.)

and they just don't end up doing it. I didn't hang out with the best crowd. I knew when I was in school that I had certain responsibilities and one responsibility was my grandmother didn't bother me as long as I did my schoolwork and was a responsible teenager. Pretty much I was allowed to be a teenager. A lot of my friends hung out and I hung out with them in places I probably shouldn't have hung out with them. But you know what, if my grandmother knew I was there she would just kill me. But one of the things that really surprised me was I remained focused regardless of my environment. A lot of my friends couldn't believe that I had my book bag with me even if we cut class or something. I couldn't take the chance of the school closing or something without getting my books.

(Kim Jones)

I didn't tell my friends that I was going to school because it was not cool and I didn't tell them I was going to college because it was not cool. Nobody knew I was going to college until—well, what happened was my grandmother took me to Boston to visit my first choice, which was Northeastern, and this was my first time out of D.C. pretty much. My teacher asked what I was going to Boston for and I said, "Well, I'm going to visit a college." He said, "I knew that but I didn't know if you were going to tell me." And he asked if I told my friends and he said he wouldn't tell anyone. But it got out and it wasn't so bad. And on graduation day they announced where I was going on scholarship and people were shocked that I was going so far and so far out of my environment. I always wanted to be a lawyer all of my life. I knew. It was really hard when my views of life changed from my friends. I didn't value driving a car and new clothes as much as my longer term goal of being self-sufficient and for longer term goals to be able to live in a comfortable manner and provide for my family in the future. It caused tension between me and my friends. It was very life changing.

(Kim Jones)

The first two years of high school, I was very introverted. My sophomore year I came out a bit. Then I tried out for this band called Malika . . . We would perform stuff like Janet Jackson or Sade or whatever was popular at the time. My best friend, Tracy, of course, she would sing. Again singing was the one thing I knew I could do. If I couldn't do anything—I was really shy—I knew I could sing. I got all the way up to the audition, they called my name and I chickened out. So I had this teacher her name was Mrs. Cole, she called me coward and all these other things and for me it didn't do anything except make me want to try out again my junior year and I was chosen. There were all these people trying out and I had such a low self-image of myself that I was like I wonder why they chose me. That band brought me out a lot. That kind of started my high school career. They would say, "Hey girl, you're in that band." We would choreograph all these steps. That's when videos just became popular and we would choreograph all these steps and play at junior high. At that time, unbeknownst to me, Me'Shell Ndegeocello was the bass player. At the time she was Michelle Johnson. At the time I had no idea she'd be this famous bass player. She was a very good bass player, but I had no idea she was going to be this famous—such an excellent bass player. Looking back at it now, I want to kick myself for having such low self-esteem

because they chose me as a singer to be alongside her. I was still very, very shy. I think I took one lead song, which was the Sade song, and that was it. But still I was in the band. It put me out there . . . We would sing a lot of assemblies. We had these little dresses with one shoulder strap and the other shoulder was out.

(Jacqueline Joyner)

I attended the Johns Hopkins University "Center for Talented Youth" program the summers after seventh or eighth grade. The program was at Dickinson College in Carlisle, Pennsylvania and that was where the Redskins practiced. A girl I knew was telling me about the great writing class, but she also told me about bumping into Joe Theisman in the cafeteria. So I took the writing class, and it really turned me on to writing. I went three straight years to take the three levels of writing.

(Danny Rose)

I went to St. Albans for grades 7 through 12. Most of my friends went on to Deal [Junior High School] and Wilson [High School]. I remember that whole process of trying to figure out which school to go to. I had gone to St. Albans for summer camp at some point in elementary school and so I remember loving it when I went to camp. Eric and Sandy both went to Deal. Sandy graduated from Wilson the same year I did. I had a lot of friends outside of Albans and I guess that made me sane. I've always been a pretty steady tennis player. I played on the tennis team at St. Albans and the football team in seventh grade, and god knows why because I'd always been a soccer player. So I played soccer and tennis at St. Albans.

(Cosby Hunt)

St. Albans is such a small place that my teachers also were friends of mine. My number one teacher was my Latin teacher Mr. Keith. Von Keith. He's probably a big part of why I'm a teacher now. He wasn't as conservative as the rest of the school. I struggled with Latin at first. I took it for four years and I remember thinking why did my parents make me take this stupid, unspoken language. Then I turned into a decent student, I started to get pretty good at translating, and I realized that this class was turning me into a good student. I would sit down and do my translation for two hours every night. I always did my Latin homework first. Mr. Keith ended up dying of AIDS. I remember him making an announcement in Last Chapel my junior year that he had AIDS and this was in 1987 around the time AIDS was becoming a big issue. The school did very well supporting him.

(Cosby Hunt)

Ms. Greene was a teacher that taught me a great deal. I had the fortune of growing up in a middle-class neighborhood and attending a wonderful, high-caliber school. I had never left Northwest D.C. I was very comfortable with my life and surroundings. I thought that since I had either grown up with or went to school with the same people for most of my life, I was familiar with the dichotomy of D.C. life. I wasn't; Ann Greene showed me this. I was the only black person in my Advanced Placement U.S. history class, the class Ms. Greene taught. One day she asked all of us to say, knowing what we know currently, how we would handle the issues of

Albert, Margot Pinkett Dyson, James Felton Ferguson, Tracy, and Brian at Tracy's graduation from the National Cathedral School, 1990. (Courtesy Tracy Ferguson.)

racism and slavery that faced state and federal legislators after the Civil War. Some classmates said they would "burn," "send away," "slaughter" those who did not fit into the majority. I was upset and repeatedly stated that we were to suggest remedies with our 20th-century knowledge. Ms. Greene made me be quiet, saying, "Now Tracy you're going to have to be quiet for the rest of the class and I don't want to hear a word out of you." I was not only angry at the rest of the class but I was even angrier at her for not stressing it is supposed to be knowing what you know now. After class, she pulled me aside and said, "Tracy, you needed to hear what was being said. You need to know that some people cannot hear what you hear, and some, some would still deal with things in ways that may shock your conscience." She

opened my eyes, taught me to listen even when I didn't like what I was hearing, and showed me that being comfortable with my surroundings was not always prudent. She was always a great teacher and then she went on to get her Ph.D. and she stands out for someone who not only made me learn but also made me learn the more monotonous things in U.S. history because she made it exciting. She made everything exciting for me. It really does depend a lot on the teacher. She made that the most exciting class I ever had.

(Tracy Ferguson)

I hated junior high because all the sudden all these things that hadn't been issues before became a big ordeal like clothes and popularity and girls—all that stuff complicated my life and I wasn't ready to

Adam and his family at the Class of 1991 Wootton High School graduation ceremony. (Courtesy Adam Vann.)

Jo Forbes Carpenter, Janet Kasdon Lobred, Damon Cordom, Susan Tassler Ginsberg, and Thaddeus Verhoff attended Woodrow Wilson High School. (Courtesy Wymer Photo Collection, HSW Collections.)

deal with that yet. Junior high was the point where I really started to swim intensely. I won meets and got to the point where I was good. Distance freestyle. There was one guy a few years younger that has since gotten better than me and he won the Olympics in 1996 . . . It wasn't affiliated with high school. It was the Rockville Montgomery Swim Club. It had private coaches. I met guys from Whitman and Churchill and met people from all the neighboring schools. It was fun. For about two years my parents had to wake up at 4:30 in the morning about three times a week before school and they had to pick me up afterwards. I got my license right at 16 so I could drive myself. In high school I started swimming a lot and I was exhausted and I would go three to four times a week and get in the water at 5 and be up at 4:30 and swim for an hour and a half and then go to high school. I had my little bagel

sandwich and eat it before class and go back again in the afternoon and swim and lift weights until about 7 o'clock at night. I was asleep through high school.

(Adam Vann)

I had Miss Carr for kindergarten. In fourth grade I wrote a letter to the National Teacher's Association supporting her nomination for teacher of the year. I felt so pleased. I struggled mightily writing that letter because I was in fourth grade but knew adults were going to read that.

(Thaddeus Marcus Verhoff)

Woodrow Wilson High School. I had a D.C. history class and it was a ninth grade thing. It was a half-year thing. The class was what you made of it. The teacher was not great but was very proud of being from D.C. At that time being proud of D.C was not very in style. "Your government is terrible, your mayor is corrupt, your roads are terrible, so what are you proud of?" he would ask us. He said the simplest thing like writing Washington, D.C. instead of writing "Wash, D.C." He talked about how U Street is very great and Duke Ellington is from D.C. It allowed me to explore D.C. Most kids weren't that interested and saw it as a joke, but I thought he was great. Mr. Winston. It is hard to develop a first name basis with your educators. They don't allow it. It was great to have someone foster such a love in your city.

(Thaddeus Marcus Verhoff)

Montessori was cool because it was open. It was not a set curriculum so you were always in command. You could do math all day and if you were really into reading books you could sit in the children's library all day, just as long as you were doing something productive and constructive. As long as you were staying busy all day and not goofing off. So I really concentrated on math. I enjoyed playing numbers games and doing long divisions and really bizarre things. I was really into it and really enjoyed it—just dividing huge numbers by other really huge numbers doing long division the old way. Unfortunately I kind of hindered my reading scores. Today I am a slow reader and I think that was the root of my problem.

(Geoffrey Koontz)

I went to the National Presbyterian School in Northwest for elementary school. I loved my kindergarten teacher because she was so sweet. They redid the school when I was there. They made a new blacktop for kickball, a new playground, and a stage in the gym for plays . . . then in fourth grade I went to the National Cathedral School. We were the otters. Ms. Bixler was an amazing

music teacher—funky and the coolest. All homerooms did a song, dance, or play for parents. I played the xylophone. For fourth grade we were in the old building. We went to the new building in sixth grade.

(Erin Marie Barringer)

I took tap and jazz until high school in Bethesda in a place called Feet First. When I was younger I went to Primary Movers on Sixteenth Street. I was a butterfly one recital. I took one year of soccer. Now I take tap and jazz at Joy of Motion in Friendship Heights. I took piano lessons in middle school by Ms. Carol Tannenwald. She lived around the block from us. I sang through school and I sang with the cellist Rostropovich at the National Cathedral School.

(Erin Marie Barringer)

Erin Marie Barringer in her backyard, 1989. (Courtesy Erin Marie Barringer.)

5. Playing around Town

We went swimming in the Mott pool up near Howard University. Where the Mott School is, that's where I learned to swim. I loved to swim. It was one of the few sports I went in for. We also played at the Mott Playground. It had a tennis court. That was about the only tennis court that we had. I have swung a racket, but I don't play a good game. There was that tennis court and the swimming pool was off to the side. There were slides and seesaws and the playground was well attended. I can't remember if there was an attendant there or not, but I remember the playground.

(Helen Combs Wood)

We went to the Smithsonian. There was just what they call the Castle. That was the Smithsonian and that's the one when you were children that you'd be taken to. And then there was a Medical Museum when I was a little older. That was down there too near the Smithsonian. I can remember going there. I remember that I was a little wheezy about the things I saw.

(Helen Combs Wood)

I remember dating and a young man would rent a car on Sundays and a group of us would go riding around and go to the Zoo and places like that. We went dancing at the Colonnade in the lower level of the Lincoln Theater on U Street. Then on Tenth and U in the Masonic Building there was a very nice dance hall there. Then in the 900 block there was a printing shop, the Murray Brothers, and upstairs was a very nice ballroom for the young set. Every Saturday there was a matinee dance . . . The White Brothers Orchestra and occasionally they would have visiting orchestras coming in. We waltzed, fox trot, jitterbug. When we went to the dances, it wasn't exactly an evening gown because it was in the afternoon. When I was an adult, I wore formal evening clothes.

(Dorothy Marita King)

Suburban Gardens was an amusement park. It had a Ferris wheel and rides. We went there by streetcar. It was quite an ordeal, but it was really a nice trip.

(Dorothy Marita King)

We played with neighborhood children at the Mott School playground at Fourth and

W Streets, NW at the Mott School. Howard University took over the playground area after awhile. We spent a lot of time as youngsters on the Howard Campus. Most of the boys loved the football and the basketball teams and we spent a lot of time there. We had free access. We did a little impromptu ball playing ourselves on the Howard diamond. We played baseball and other games that I can't remember.

(Frank R. Jackson)

I spent a lot of time around the river. Around those days corporal punishment was accepted as a form of controlling children. Growing up I got more whippings for going down to the Tidal Basin than for any other reason that I can remember. But I loved going down to the river all the way up to Hains Point and then all the way up into the Tidal Basin and up the Potomac to the Chain Bridge. I knew that river from between those points. I had a couple of buddies who I did it with: Russell "Piggy" Banks, three brothers named King, and my real ace buddy Harry Robbins and we called him "Happy." So that was fun. We caught little perch about six inches long and sometimes catfish about a foot long, which was big for us kids.

(Frank R. Jackson)

We had three theaters on U Street: the Booker T, the Republic, and the Lincoln. The Lincoln, of course, is still standing. We enjoyed first-class films in those three theaters. The Howard Theater had big acts. Of course I didn't get to go to the Howard

A dance at the Lincoln Colonnade, 1930s. (Courtesy Robert H. McNeill.)

Fishing along East Potomac Park. (Courtesy Wymer Photo Collection, HSW Collections.)

Marion Jackson Pryde outside of her house at 1533 T Street, NW, 1928. (Courtesy Marion Jackson Pryde.)

very often because it was very expensive and younger children didn't go.

(Marion Jackson Pryde)

My Uncle Harry took me to my first baseball game. [The Senators] played the New York Giants and all the big leagues. I sat in the bleachers of Griffith Stadium all the way in the back. I used to be crazy about it. I'd go any chance I could. Oh, I used to go in the days when little kids could be taken for nothing. So when my father lived at Sixth and K, NE, he used to take me down to the stadium and I used to go up to someone and say, "Mister, will you please take me into the game with you?" I'd hold his hand and go into the game and my father or mother would come down and pick me up after the game. So that's how I got into the games as a little kid.

(Robert Israel Silverman)

Skating around the Washington Monument, 1935. (Courtesy HSW Collections, CHS 6974.)

I had a lot of cousins. They'd close up the grocery store on Sundays and they'd put the kids in the back of the car and we'd go to Rock Creek Park or we'd go to Potomac Park. We'd call it the Speedway—that was East Potomac Park. Potomac River was on one side and Hains Point was down there. The kids would play ball all the time and the women would bring the cooking with them and they'd have open-air grills in the park. The women got together and the kids got together and were running around and jumping around—these kids who later became such prominent people in Washington. We went to the Speedway and Rock Creek Park . . . There was no television and you couldn't afford to go to baseball games. I became a football fan. Another thing we did was go to the theater. There'd be a Yiddish Theater, the Belasco Theater. It faced Lafayette Park on the east side of the street. The whole theater would be filled up with Jewish people and there'd

be comedies and they were funny. I'd go to some of them. I understood the language partially. It broke up the monotony of living.

(Robert Israel Silverman)

There weren't too many boys and I played the saxophone in the band. My father got me an alto. Eventually I had two or three saxophones and I played in the school band and played at dances in school and outside. My buddy went to Tech High and he organized a band. He had a touring car. His name was Thompson. He'd come and pick me up. I couldn't have been any more than 14 or 15 years old. We played at some dance way down in Virginia. Guess where? In Alexandria. My mother thought it was somewhere on the other side of the world.

(Robert Israel Silverman)

We were in close proximity to the Mall and we relished the opportunity to go the museums down there. We knew every crevice and corner in the museums and took advantage of that. We were privileged to have that facility [the museums and monuments] so close so we could take advantage of it. We got to know where almost every exhibit was. We probably would have been good tour guides. We considered the Mall our park. We used to try to pick a baseball game up there and police would come and chase us off. There was a motorcycle police officer and when he'd come on the scene and the kids saw him coming, they'd dash off. Sometimes they may have dropped a baseball or ball and glove. He'd pick it up, put it in his sidecar, and drive away.

(Joseph Eugene Zeis)

The Army Medical Museum was on Seventh Street and Independence Avenue, NW. It was exciting for kids to go in there. We saw some strange things in the Army Medical Museum. They had a general's leg and other bizarre things. We used to go in there before they restricted your visit according to your age. It was kind of fascinating when I told other kids we went. We'd go with kids and not parents. We were trusted to go to the park or the museums, the Mall area.

(Joseph Eugene Zeis)

We lived near the intersection of Pennsylvania Avenue and whenever we heard of a parade, my sister Freida and I would go to the grocery store and salvage wooden crates. We would rent the crates for 10¢ to short people who wanted to see the floats and bands coming up the avenue. People would stand for ten minutes or so, and then give the crates back. We would rent them to the next person. We made

A circus parade on Pennsylvania Avenue, around where Markus Ring lived and played. (Courtesy HSW Collections, CHS 2263.)

enough money that my father took the money to the Old Lincoln National Bank and opened up a savings account. That was the start of our fortune.

(Markus Ring)

On the southwest corner of Seventeenth and Pennsylvania Avenue was the Mills Building built by General Mills of the Civil War. After the war he invented a belt that had space for ammunition and supplies. He made so much money off that, he built the building. On top of the building was a flagpole. Because there was no radio, if the Senators won, one type of flag went up and if they lost another went up. The losing flag was up there most of the time and that's how we found out how the Senators got along. July 4, 1933 they played a double header with the New York Yankees and I saw Babe Ruth put one over the right field

fence and I was there with a half dozen boys and we were hollering and yelling as he rounded third base. He always took his cap off for a thank you for the applause.

(Markus Ring)

As far as theater, young people weren't really exposed to culture. My parents were busy making a living. We used to go to old Griffith Stadium for baseball games at Seventh and Florida Avenues, NW. [Walter] Johnson was my favorite player then. Radios were very scarce then. The gas station across the street from the store had the only radio so we got to listen to the game on the radio. Everybody in the neighborhood was around the radio listening to the World Series. I got the thrill of watching Babe Ruth hit a ball over the center field fence at Griffith Stadium. He pointed to it. That was the famous pointing

White and black Washingtonians attended events at Griffith Stadium. (Courtesy HSW Collections, CHS 4749.)

game. There was a bakery next door to Griffith Stadium. It was a branch of the Continental Baking Company, a very large bakery, and you could smell it all the way up Georgia Avenue—it was a good bakery with a very pleasant smell.

(Marvin Tievsky)

We picnicked in Rock Creek Park. We used to go down to the Smithsonian. My uncle had a store in Southwest near the museums. When we visited him on Saturdays and [the store] was open late, we would go to a different museum. There was the Army Medical Museum and as a young boy it was very interesting. They had pickled embryos and tropical diseases that you didn't hear about until World War II. I remember when they opened the National Gallery of Art and when they opened the Shakespeare Museum in 1932 behind the

Library of Congress, the Folger Theater. I think I was there the first week they opened. The [Smithsonian] Castle was still there and they had one other building. The dinosaur building was also great.

(Marvin Tievsky)

The arrival of the circus every spring was an exciting event. When the Ringling Bros. and Barnum & Bailey show would come in a few days early, it would set up tents at an outlying site before moving to the exhibition grounds on Bladensburg Road. In the year they encamped near Falls Church, Virginia, my buddies talked me into hitchhiking there to see what we could do to earn some tickets for the Big Top. To our delight, one of the handlers let us carry water for the elephants and gave each of us a ticket for admission to the show on the next Saturday. I don't know which was

Austin Kiplinger on a pony and wagon, a common type of photograph for the children of Washington, 1923. (Courtesy Kiplinger Archives.)

Flora Blumenthal Atkin celebrating her birthday with friends on Klingle Road, c. 1926. *(Courtesy Flora Blumenthal Atkin.)*

more exciting—the show or watering the elephants.

(Austin Kiplinger)

My sister and I, when she got a bit older, did a lot of things together. Eleanor was her name. We played paper dolls in the sunroom that joined our two bedrooms in the back. We would put 40 or 50 paper dolls on the floor and leave them there for days and make clothes for them. We would say, well, today they are going to a party so we would make party dresses for every single one of the dolls. And the next day they were going somewhere cold and we made coats for them, etc. In the hot summer we would go to the attic and there was no air conditioning in there at the time. It was sweltering up there and we would stay up there until we were really hot. I mean water was just dripping down us and then we would run down to the second floor, run down to the first floor, run down to the basement, and then lie on the cement floor. It was our own personal sauna that we created.

(Flora Blumenthal Atkin)

"O'Leary. One, two, three, O'Leary." You bounced a medium rubber ball and on the word O'Leary you put your foot over it. "One, two, three, O'Leary. Four, five, six, O'Leary. Seven, eight, nine, O'Leary. Ten O'Leary postmen." There were variations. Sometimes you clapped underneath when the ball went under it, double bouncer, two legs over it, swing your leg over the other way, the other leg, stamping with it. There were 20 or 30 variations. That was a game we played by the hour. You practiced by yourself and made sure you were good at it and then played with other kids.

(Flora Blumenthal Atkin)

Chevy Chase Lake was sort of the end of the world. It was a real outing to go all the way to Chevy Chase Lake. They had dancing at Chevy Chase Lake and at Glen

103

Echo. I don't know if the pool was at Chevy Chase yet. Even before I went dancing at Glen Echo when I was 18, we would just ride the cars and go and sit under the trees and have a lunch.

(Janet Kasdon Lobred)

We played ball in the back alley and Bancroft School was a half a block away. Rock Creek Park was on the other side of Ingleside Terrace, and we used to go down the hill and several of us built a cave and covered it over with stuff. It was like Tom Sawyer and we were kids.

(Leonard Lobred)

I was wild about all sports. Baseball at Griffith Stadium. To get ladies there, they had a Ladies Day and men always had to pay. We didn't pay much just $1 or $1.10 to go. I have autographed baseballs from that period: Walter Johnson, Carl Reynolds, Lou

Gehrig. I had an uncle by marriage who was a pitcher for the Boston Braves and he gave me a ball with some autographs. I wanted to be a sportswriter and was for the high school weekly and the college daily. By the time I graduated college, I did not want to be a sportswriter. I had already seen too much professionalism and I was just completely turned off.

(Leonard Lobred)

Kids danced a lot back then. We would dance on the streets. One of the guys on the block played an accordion but mostly we danced to the radio. We had a makeshift record player in our house. We had huge dances during the summer nights. There would be two policeman and about 800 kids dancing. It was all segregated, of course. This was all white kids. We went three or four times a week and we loved the dances. I learned to

Frolicking around Rock Creek Park, c. 1920. (Courtesy Photo Album #12, HSW Collections.)

Richard Hawes walking downtown on a Saturday afternoon, 1942. (Courtesy Richard Hawes.)

Florence Crawford Marvil at Hains Point with her younger sister Emilie, 1931. (Courtesy Florence Crawford Marvil.)

dance the jitterbug and swing from my sister and her girlfriends because they were two years older.

(Richard E. Hawes)

We used to live at the movies. The Silver and Newton Theaters were only seven or eight blocks away. On Saturdays we went downtown to F Street. That's where we saw stage shows for 25¢. We went to the Earle, which is now the Warner Theater, and the Palace near F and Thirteenth—that played the best movies in town, but it didn't have stage shows. There was also the Fox and then the Capitol was where the Press Club is now. Sometimes we would walk down. For 25¢ you saw a movie, coming attractions, and a stage show—big name bands or comedians who were probably too sophisticated for us, but we laughed

anyway. I was probably seven or eight when I started going to the theaters. Kids would all go together in groups. We felt safe. We might ride the streetcar and often we might skate. Downtown movies were only on weekends. My sister and I went at night in our neighborhood because my parents loved to play cards. As a matter of fact a lot of the men that worked in the railroad from my neighborhood would play cards at night. We'd do our homework and then go to the movies. I think I saw as many movies as a kid as any kid in my block and I'm still a movie buff.

(Richard E. Hawes)

I was a goody goody and friends of mine were the troublemakers because they were fun. One day a friend talked me into going to the drugstore with her during lunch, which we goody goodies would never do, but she talked me into it. Thus I went with her and we came back three minutes late and the assistant principal was waiting for me, and he said, "I'm so disappointed in you Florence," and I died a thousand deaths. Of course I never did anything like that again. It was on the corner of Fourteenth and Clifton. That's where all the fun people went for lunch.

(Florence Crawford Marvil)

On Friday afternoons my aunt would take us down to the polo fields on the Mall to watch polo games. This was Aunt Josephine. She didn't have any children and wasn't married. Many, many, many weekends the family had picnics in Rock Creek Park. Someone in the family would call to reserve an area and we would have picnics there. My sister and I as tiny children were taken to Meridian Hill to play and back then she was called a mother's helper, but now she would be called a nanny. There was a group of men who had a croquet club and they would come every afternoon after their work to play croquet. Those wickets stayed up all summer long. We children never touched them. Those croquet mallets laid in boxes under benches and we children never touched them. If our ball was to roll over on their croquet part, we'd be horrified and gently whispered to one of the men to throw it back to us. We would never think of that today. This croquet set was set up all summer long and no one ever touched the mallets under the benches.

(Florence Crawford Marvil)

Back then it was customary for parents to let their daughters give tea parties. The girls would come dressed in white gloves and would come on the weekends and they had hats and we had tea sandwiches, tea, and cookies. Families entertained each other that way. Also that's how you entertained other people who you didn't go to school with because, remember, I went to church downtown.

(Florence Crawford Marvil)

After my father got a car we would go to the Speedway where the Kennedy Center is now. We spread a blanket out and watched the planes and the boats. That's what we did on Sunday afternoon. We drove around the city to see new things being built. We went to Suburban Gardens on the streetcar. It was similar to Glen Echo. It was at the end of the line and then you had to get on the bus. Life was simple. You didn't have any money so you did the simplest of things. You didn't need a lot of money.

(Clara Sharon Taylor)

On the comics page we read *Mescal Ike*, *Mutt and Jeff*, *Bringing up Father*, *Smokey Stover*, and the *Katzenjammer Kids*, a name I learned very much later in life when I knew some German, means yowling cats. And in about 1930 we got our first radio, an Atwater-Kent with four stations: WRC, WMAL, WOLA, and WJSV, stations which are still in operation, although I believe WJSV exchanged its name. I was told there was a station in Pittsburgh called KDKA, which I refused to believe. Radio stations began with W! We were given the radio a few days "on approval" and one of the children's programs was *The Lady Next Door*. I was listening to it one evening when the man from the store came to take the radio away, and I think it was the only time in my life I ever threw a temper tantrum. My parents' assurance that we were going to get a radio permanently and I could listen to the program as often as I wanted did nothing to soothe me. I wanted to hear it now!

(Jo Forbes Carpenter)

I discovered baseball, both attending the games and listening to the broadcasts by announcer Arch MacDonald. Out of town games did not have direct transmission but had to be telegraphed in, so one heard several minutes of clicking and then Mr. McDonald repeating the plays. Everyone in those days thought it was rather strange that a girl child would be interested in baseball; little did they know that it was the players more than the game that stirred me. Buddy Lewis and Cecil Travis were my special heroes, but I also remember a great galumphing first baseman named Zeke Bonura and a plump little Cuban outfielder Bobby Estalella. There was another Buddy, Buddy Myer, who sparked the only brawl I think the Senators ever had when he spiked a rival second baseman. And of course the brothers Rick and Wes Ferrell who were catcher and pitcher . . . I also attended an opening game, it must have been somewhere in his third term, to see FDR throw out the first ball. It amazes me that at the time and for years afterwards I, like most of the country, had no idea that he could not walk or stand without assistance. Although I never met any of my heroes, as a junior at Woodrow Wilson High School I was assigned to interview a well-known person. I chose the manager of the Senators, Bucky Harris, a delightful man who very cordially agreed to be interviewed and met me in his office, a rather dingy little room in the equally dingy Griffith Stadium. After the interview he took me out on the field to see what it looked like from the players' point of view. One of my life's real thrills!

(Jo Forbes Carpenter)

Jo Forbes Carpenter on a stone wall at the south side of Wilson High School, 1942. (Courtesy Jo Forbes Carpenter.)

Saturday afternoons were spent at the movies. We would take a bus, which left from Tenley Circle, called the Crosstown Bus and go to the Avalon Theater, where we would see a program consisting of a newsreel; a cartoon; a one-reeler, which frequently featured Edgar Kennedy; sometimes a Travelogue; the main feature; and, of course, a serial cliffhanger such as Buck Rogers or Flash Gordon. Films did not have designated times but ran continuously with a program usually beginning about 1 o'clock—giving rise to the expression "This is where I came in." About 6 o'clock the serial was taken off but the rest of the program continued until about 11 . . . I remember going to the Capitol, the Keith's, and the Earle Theaters where there was always a variety show on stage. My very first movie I saw at the age of four was called *Way Out West* and starred William Haines and Leila Hyams. There was a scene where he rescued her from a rattlesnake and playing this scene at home was a great entertainment for me, being sometimes the hero, sometimes the heroine, and sometimes the snake.

(Jo Forbes Carpenter)

After school activities, besides musical ones, were bowling at the Ice Palace, which was both a skating rink and bowling alley . . . hamburgers at the Hot Shoppe on Wisconsin Avenue and shopping at Sears-

Charlie Brotman learning to walk outside his home in the Eckington neighborhood, c. 1928. (Courtesy Charlie Brotman.)

Roebuck at the corner of Wisconsin Avenue and Albemarle Street were also within walking distance of school.

(Jo Forbes Carpenter)

We loved to dance the jitterbug in the store. Our customers enjoyed it and thought it was so much fun. We had an alley behind the store. The top of the street was a hill and they ultimately put apartments there, but kids used to play when it was a hill. The guys would play football and basketball. We'd also go to Edgewood or Langley Junior High playgrounds. We'd wrap up the daily paper in the shape of a football or baseball and got a broom handle. We went to the playground for basketball. We also played kick the can and tag. There was a camaraderie of the neighborhood. We'd create games. We'd go to the telephone directory and look up exchanges—it wasn't all numbers, but something like North 2487. We'd each take a name and go through the directory to see who had the most names.

(Charles Brotman)

After school you played sports and then got home dog-tired and would eat dinner and do homework. You didn't have time after school. I don't remember Georgetown being that attractive to us on the weekends. We had a sister school, Cathedral, and Mount Vernon School, which were all girls schools. Northwest stayed pretty much in Northwest except trips to play other kids. We came downtown on the weekends to see the movies and the big bands perform. There wasn't much in the way of nightlife. The big social place was the Hot Shoppes on Connecticut Avenue, just above the Bureau of Standards where UDC is now. Everyone met there with their A&W root beers. That's where everybody met after

Opening day of the 4300 Connecticut Avenue Hot Shoppe, 1940. (Courtesy Marriott International Inc.)

the games. Games were on Friday afternoons. Sometimes fights broke out between the boys in private and public school. We would all go in whatever cars we could use—a lot of jalopies—and meet there on Friday and Saturday nights.

(George Ferris Jr.)

My brother Sam and I were friendly and we would attend the Redskins game [at Griffith Stadium]. You could get in for $4 or $5. When I was about 16 I would walk with Sam on F Street and go to the Capitol Theater or the Earle Theater and for $1 you could see a movie and a vaudeville show. We saw Benny Goodman there and many other comedians and other acts. The Palace and the Keith's were others. We'd walk around F Street and we did that for quite awhile.

(Larry Rosen)

I went to Center Camp at the JCC that just came back. They used to have dances there. As I grew older, I did more there: dances and plays. The Nye House in Southwest was more active and closer. They had Sunday school and ping pong games. Boys Club #4 was on I Street between Fourth and Sixth.

(Larry Rosen)

I had a very fortunate childhood. I regard Burleith as a special place because of it. It's close to everything yet it's a quiet place . . . We had a little gang at Burleith. My chief friends were Randy Watson, Eddie Sylvester, Bucky and Chuck Molster. Eddie and Bucky are still in the area. As a group we would do things like go to the movies. At various times we had teams like football teams called the Burleith Panthers. We would play up in an area called the

Larry Rosen and his cousin Leslie Cohen in Southwest, c. 1932. (Courtesy Larry Rosen.)

Greenfields. It's a little park going west from Thirty-seventh above T Street . . . We went biking, to the movies. We played tag when we were younger and Red Rover Come Over. We played across the street because the traffic was nil. The street was our boundary. We played hide 'n seek.

(Myles MacCrimmon Johnson)

You could pretty easily go down to Glen Echo. You'd pick up the trolley and go along the river up to Glen Echo. In the early days they still had the open streetcars so you could sit on the outside like they have in San Francisco. That was a great ride. We'd go and spend all day. If it rained we'd spend the day inside at the activities. It was a stone building. The stone was a major attraction. It was a huge pool and, of course, it was the reason Glen Echo was shut down—because they didn't allow blacks in and then there were protests. It was a stupid policy. In the early '50s there were protests and they preferred to close the place than bow to protests.

(Myles MacCrimmon Johnson)

I was rather stupid in not taking advantage of the live shows when I was younger, but when I got to be high school age I went to see Louis Armstrong's group down on Fourteenth Street. That was tremendous. It was a small room very long and narrow and the band played on a little ledge behind the bar and I was seated at the bar. It was fascinating to see the drummer. It was marvelous. I went with a friend named Bob Travis and probably with Warren Roberts.

(Myles MacCrimmon Johnson)

We went swimming in the summer at Glen Echo and there was a close public pool at Volta Park, but we never went there. I went at my high school. One place we went to was technically illegal was behind Georgetown University there's a deep valley. It's sort of filled in now. They had a pool in Georgetown University—they had a pool and I think it was for staff. We used to climb over the fence and go swimming there. This was with my friends.

(Myles MacCrimmon Johnson)

Dances were fun because even the kids in Southeast went. During that time we were limited to schools because of segregation. I only really remember Randall Junior High but I got to know kids from all over the city. They would come to the rec center. It was just fun walking, and talking, and playing around. We would pick up kids along the way and it was real nice.

(Mary Meade Coates)

We used to go to Howard for their terrific stage shows: Pearl Bailey, James Brown

Myles MacCrimmon Johnson at 3829 S Street, NW in his cadet uniform, 1945. (Courtesy Myles MacCrimmon Johnson.)

came later, Milo Hampton. My neighbor used to play the piano. Other theaters were the Howard, the Broadway, the Lincoln Theater, and the Republic. The Jewell and Rosalia were in Southwest. We would go on Saturdays for the serials and the movies and get to stay all day. Later came the Senator in Northeast. The Howard Theater was the main one. It had live shows and then we would stay. We then caught the bus and went home. It went straight down Seventh Street.

(Mary Meade Coates)

We played several games. One with an ice pick that we played in a tree box in the dirt. We would sit and there were different ways you threw this in the dirt. I can't remember

111

A view taken from Myles MacCrimmon Johnson's backyard at 3829 S Street, across Western High Stadium to Georgetown University towers, 1941. (Courtesy Myles MacCrimmon Johnson.)

all the things and how they went. If your ice pick fell, you lost your turn. There were jacks, hopscotch, and marbles. These were things we played all our lives and we just continued into the young teenage years. We played hopscotch. Sundays were real good days because people got bus passes and we went to the colored pawn, which was on the other side of South Capitol Street just near M. We'd go there and buy the passes from them. A couple of kids under 12 could ride the buses for free with the passes and we would ride all over the city. We would bring the pass back to the person we bought it from and go home.

(Mary Meade Coates)

We all looked forward to getting out of school and then we didn't know what to do with ourselves. We played baseball. The lot

had debris and broken glass. We would clean it and get cardboard bases or use our sweatshirts. We would play kick the can and hide 'n go seek. Because some of the boys would not be around, we would permit some of the girls who lived in the apartment house to play. People didn't talk too much of vacations because the money wasn't there. We would pack picnic baskets and go to Hains Point and have an outing there.

(Damon Cordom)

My mother liked the theater a lot. We went to what was considered the neighborhood theater, which was at Twenty-first and Pennsylvania Avenue. I remember paying 9¢ to get in. I had a friend who went with me one day and we found out the price got raised to 11¢. That angered us because we didn't have the extra pennies, so we went around looking for coat hangers and soft drink bottles to turn in somewhere to get the additional 2¢. I don't think we found them.

(Damon Cordom)

We bought a nice little row house in Congress Heights at 403 Oakwood Street, SE. I would have been six when that happened. I went to Congress Heights Elementary School and walked to school. Congress Heights was like a little town. We had a movie theater called the Congress Theater at the intersection of Nichols Avenue and Portland Street and some of my strongest recollections are of going to the movies every Saturday. There were six neighborhood boys, Pat Kober, Russell Duffy, Gene Bowersox, Ross Hudson, and Wayne Vipon, and we did everything together . . . Our mothers gave us a quarter and I can remember paying 17¢ for the movie. Each one of us would pool our 3¢ to buy a sack of honey-dipped doughnuts at the neighborhood bakery on the same block as the movie theater. With the nickel we would buy some kind of candy that would last us through two movies, a serial, a cartoon, and the news. We'd sit there for three or four hours and normally it was a cowboy movie or a serial, another movie, a short with the *Three Stooges* or *Our Gang*, a cartoon or two, and then the news. We went to the theater at 1 and then we would walk back home together. Whatever the movie was that day, we would replay on the walk home.

(Tom Reese)

Damon Cordom in front of cherry blossoms, 1937. (Courtesy Damon Cordom.)

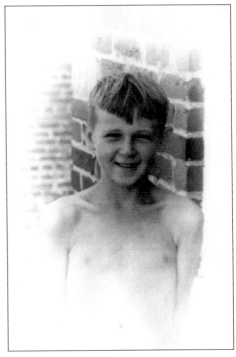

Tom Reese after a long day of playing, 1942. (Courtesy Tom Reese.)

The candy store we went to was People's Drug Store, which was at the corner of Portland Street across the street from the Congress Theater. They had a soda fountain and our favorite sundae was chocolate ice cream with marshmallow sauce. It was served in a beautiful pressed steel sundae glass, which would be so cold because they kept it in the freezer box. It was just marvelous. It cost 15¢, which was a little much for us, so we didn't get that very often. We tried to get a lot of money together so each of us could get our own. We collected bottles to trade in for money. The soda bottles were 2¢ and the quart bottles were a nickel. We tried to collect them and take them to the supermarket. Around construction sites were a real good place to find bottles because the construction workers didn't turn the bottles back in and there was a lot of construction in our neighborhood during World War II to try and accommodate the people coming to work for the government. We would buy candy or soda with the money or whatever we wanted to do that day.

(Tom Reese)

We had three black movie houses we could attend—the Lincoln, the Republic, and the Booker T. We used to love to go there in the summertime. We had to carry a jacket and we would stay in there all day long because back then there weren't many poor colored with air conditioning . . . We went to the movies every Saturday. If you had show passes you only paid 7¢ to get into the movie and then popcorn was 10¢. Popcorn was more than the movie. Then in the afternoon we used to go to the movies a lot of the time, especially in the middle of the summer.

(Lillie Latten)

In the heart of U Street, the Republic Theater showed first run films to the African-American community. (Courtesy Wymer Photo Collection, HSW Collections.)

Flora Atkin and Susan Ginsberg recall going to movies at the Tivoli Theater on Fourteenth Street. (Courtesy Wymer Photo Collection, HSW Collections.)

I went to the Savoy and the Tivoli, and on Fourteenth Street, the Ambassador Theater on Eighteenth and Columbia Road and the Ontario Theater in the '50s. That was exciting when it opened. I remember skipping a class to go there and see a movie, which was very unusual of me [to skip class] and I just ducked down and hoped no teacher was doing the same.

(Susan Tassler Ginsberg)

Every Saturday my little ritual was this: they had these chapters like Zorro and cowboy movies. I would stop at a place that sold ice cream and I'd get a half pint of ice cream. Then I'd stop at a place called the Chicken Box and get the best hot dog in the world. They sold hot dogs that were better than at the movies. They also sold French fries and I got those. Then I'd go into the theater and I'd buy sodas, and I stayed in the

theater all day because you could. Then I'd go home and play.

(James Davis)

We would trade cards or play games like Pitch Cards where we would pitch cards against the wall and whoever came the closest won. Wing Cards, they were photos of airplanes, and as you got older there were experimental aircrafts and jet airplanes. They would always come with a slab of pink bubblegum that we would chew. It was awful, but we'd chew it anyway and we had so many cavities. Sometimes we would just throw the gum against a lamppost and it would splatter into a thousand pieces, it was so stale.

(Sandy Berk)

On Saturdays we would go to the triple feature in the summer. We would go to the

Sandy Berk attended the Beverly Theater in Northeast Washington. (Courtesy Wymer Photo Collection, HSW Collections.)

Kennedy around 12 and not be seen again until about 6 o'clock . . . We would walk to the Kennedy. It was a long walk but we would do it. We started at 7 or 8 and it was a few miles. Favorite movies were cartoons, swashbuckling movies, pirates, cowboy movies, war movies. We hated the mushy ones especially when there were lots of kissing scenes and then just a few acting scenes. They had yo-yo contests during intermission. We would go there in the summer for the air conditioning. Someone would drive us if it was cold or rainy. In the summer it would feel so hot when we stepped out of the theater after spending the day in there.

(Sandy Berk)

I don't remember doing extracurriculars in elementary school. I don't know if they existed then. Kids got out of school and they went and they played and had a wonderful time. They didn't take skating lessons and judo and all the stuff they do now. We just played and had fun . . . When we moved out to Wheaton there were still a lot of woods and we would play in the woods. Then we used to play hopscotch and hide and seek. I guess we must have biked a lot. It was quite a community spirit there. The kids I went to school with I saw after school and the kids from the neighborhood. It was a very cohesive community. Where I lived was a development and it was safe, extremely safe. Mothers would let their children out in the morning and not worry about where they were until it was time to come home for dinner. I am sure if I was eating lunch over a friend's house I was supposed to say that I was eating there. But I could say I am going to play in the woods all day and she would never worry about me, at least to the best of my knowledge. So we had free range of the neighborhood that was probably a mile from one end to the other. Hundreds and hundreds and hundreds of houses and nobody ever worried. It was a whole different world. My children never had that much freedom and kids today don't have that much freedom. It was a whole different world. It was incredible.

(Sally Lichtenstein Berk)

I was a great softball player in the neighborhood. There was an alleyway, but also in the center of neighborhood was a small field. It seemed large at the time. That's where we played. I was a tomboy. I played field hockey in junior high and we played against other schools . . . I couldn't go swimming at Coolidge without my cousins. We all had to go together. We all went swimming together.

(Gretchen Roberts-Shorter)

We used to go to Glen Echo. I loved that. I'd go on the rides. I used to go bowling and to the movies. The bowling alley was on Westwood beyond Western Avenue. Actually there is a bowling alley where Fresh Fields is . . . We went to the Hot Shoppes for lunch. That was fun. There was one in Van Ness. We went to the Avalon Theater. We took dancing lessons above the Avalon Theater . . . I took piano lessons with Ms. Winston on Appleton Street. I went to friend's houses and we'd play. I took singing too and at camp I used to perform plays.

(Alison Luchs)

Opal was my best friend in high school. Opal and I did the movies. Opal did the party circuit and I wasn't big on the party circuit. We went to see *Bye Bye Birdie* with Ann Margaret on New York Avenue. The theater was sort of a donation from my aunt as an enrichment experience . . . and it also wasn't a bad way to keep tabs on me. Opal went to Taft for two years and became a Catholic in eighth grade and decided she wanted to go to Catholic school. Her parents were not Catholic. It's an interesting story how Opal became Catholic. She went to CCD class with her friend Rosemary, because CCD was held right before the 1 o'clock matinee at the Newton, and they went to the movies afterward. She had no real reason to go to CCD, but the ride was only going one time. Opal and I were in the same theater at the same time, but we didn't know each other until we got to high school. We were in the same neighborhood realm but never met up because we went to such different schools until high school. We attended the Academy of Our Lady High School. It's part of St. Cecilia's now. I was on the 80 bus for 40 minutes. I would meet Opal and she lived at the end of the line so she would save me a seat. Even if she couldn't save a seat for me, she would help me hold my books because it was hard to stand up and hold on and carry books. I had a purse and my books—backpacks were not around.

(Mary Teresa Barrick Stilwell)

My mother played tent and store with us. She was our best customer and we played bank with her typewriter, because she did typing at home for extra money. She used to take us to the movies in the summer because Washington was not air conditioned except for the movies and the department stores. She would take us to the theater and she would sleep in the air conditioning knowing we would not leave the theater. She had a nice nap and then at night with the window fan breeze she would type because she got a good rest in the afternoon. So that's how she managed to work through the summers to get the typing done on people's dissertations. She was a clever woman and it was relatively inexpensive in those days—it was probably 30¢ apiece.

(Mary Teresa Barrick Stilwell)

Opal and I went to Meisner's and Murphy's. If you wanted a record you needed to go to a record store. Meisner's had three floors and a lunch counter. Meisner's was like a small Wal-Mart except it had some specialty items. You bought jewelry only at jewelry stores. They had a market at Meisner's with groceries. There were chickens hanging up and lots of fresh food. It was different when I went in because we were used to dime stores with notions departments but never one big store. So we would go to Meisner's and have a little snack and then hit the record store and pick up my Motown and Opal's Bob Dylan. She did the Beatles and I did Smokey [Robinson]. It was funny because she was black and we somehow got mixed in our tastes—it was like opposite of what it should have been.

(Mary Teresa Barrick Stilwell)

Mary Teresa Barrick Stilwell's graduating class from Academy of Our Lady High School on Fifth and G Place, NW, 1966. (Courtesy Mary Teresa Barrick Stilwell.)

Downtown along F Street. (Courtesy Wymer Photo Collection, HSW Collections.)

My dad built us all a stage where we could do the marionette thing. Ms. Allen, when she found out about this, said, "Well, this is just fabulous. We are going to combine this with some musical entertainment and we are going to go down to Chinatown." The script was bizarre because how you fit a hillbilly into a Cinderella story, I don't know. And the other thing is that it was a big Chinese audience and I am pretty sure most of them didn't understand English. But they seemed to enjoy themselves. So that was interesting.

(Timothy Burton)

I remember sledding down Westover Drive heading straight towards Pennsylvania Avenue. And I look at this now and think how could our parents let us do this. We used to have 20 or 30 kids all with our Flexible Flyers and our little metal dishes and we'd be going as fast as we could down

that steep hill and right before Pennsylvania Avenue turn left and down to an open field. That's what we would do from morning to evening and sometimes after dinner! It was the whole neighborhood and then when it turned to ice that was the best. None of us got killed, which was amazing. My dad did take us once to 295 and next to where they were digging were huge hills. He took us tobogganing there when they were still in the process of building.

(Judy Scott Feldman)

Kids were really independent back then. We could walk to school by ourselves back then. We used to play in the woods right at Branch and Penn. We also used to walk through Fort David Park on the way to the Fort David Library on Saturdays and sometimes I would do it all by myself even when I was ten. I also remember going to some woods near Branch and Penn when I

Judy Scott Feldman helping with the dishes, 1954. (Courtesy Judy Scott Feldman.)

Jacque Joyner looking shy, c. 1975. (Courtesy Jacque Joyner.)

was about ten. We'd find sewer pipes that ran under the roads. We used to take tiny little birthday candles, we didn't tell anybody, and we'd light them and we'd walk through the pipes and it would be such an adventure. We burned the spider webs and things inside. These sewer pipes were probably four feet high and we would go to one neighborhood to the other and all we knew was that we had to be home by 5. My mother would blow a whistle. We couldn't hear it down there, but we knew. We were famous for the whistle. In the whole neighborhood, the first blow meant get ready to come home we're going to eat and the second blow, two short blows in a row, meant quick you got to be here in 30 seconds because we are going to sit down. So everybody knew the Scott whistle. If you didn't hear it, they would all tell you. We were regimented like the military in our

house. And then in our house we had the bell. The one bell meant wash your hands and the second bell meant sit at the table. It started with the whistles and then the bells. Then after dinner we would say the rosary. We would always kneel at the table and say the rosary. After dinner the kids would come to the house because we were supposed to go back out and play, and the kids would all stand at the window and say, "They're saying their prayers again." They'd all be peeking in and we'd be saying our prayers.

(Judy Scott Feldman)

We went to the park on Madison Street and Kansas Avenue, NW—Fort Slocum Park. That's one of the places we would go to fly kites in the spring. We would explore in the wooded areas. We would roll down the hills in the spring and summer and in the winter

120

we made makeshift sleds out of cardboard or get plastic round discs and sled down the hill in the winter.

(Andrea Littlejohn)

[We went to] Tom's Candy Store on the 100 block of Kennedy Street. He sold a lot of penny candy. We went after school. Some would go during school at lunch. Penny candy was like Squirrel Nuts, which was a type of caramel candy and it had coconut and syrup. It was a syrup with shredded coconut rolled in orange and red wrappers. The candy was no thicker than a pencil. Then kisses, which was hard candy in different flavors. Lemonheads, which was sour. Bubblegum balls. We'd also buy bat balls, the paddle with the ball attached. We played jacks and double dutch. Double dutch was very popular among elementary school girls. We played in the streets or in the alleys. We played kickball in the alleys. We also played hide 'n go seek and played tag where someone was designated "it," chase after other kids, and tag the kid and whoever got tagged was the next person to be "it." Going to the park, playing in the street, playing in the alley, and walking to and from the store made up a large part of our activities.

(Andrea Littlejohn)

I've seen the Smithsonian a lot and practically grew up there. Unless they have moved things, I can tell you where everything is. I can tell you where the dinosaurs are and I can tell you where the Hope Diamond is and the statue of George Washington. I know how to go in and out of all those buildings. My parents took me to the museums until I got to the age where I could go around by myself.

(Desmond Leary)

I don't know how long the mall phenomenon has existed, but I feel like I discovered the mall. D.C. is surrounded by suburbs and I would go to many: Mazza Gallery, PG Plaza, Chevy Chase Malls. We were all over. Malls were a place for girl watching and book reading and hanging out. I discovered the guitar at the mall because there used to be a Harmony Hut place. I remember it had a record store and an instrument store and I remember going into that place for about a year and buying records. It was about eight miles from my house. We drove, but we walked when my mom wasn't home because eight miles isn't really that long when you have a record to buy. The first album my mother bought me was a spoken word album.

(Keith Lofton)

One thing I liked about D.C. is we got snow. That is something I wished for back in L.A., especially at Christmas. Winters were great. The first winter we were here my father bought Brian and me a sled. We lived on top of a hill and all the kids would come over to sled. There was this enclosure of bushes and we needed to break through the bushes in order to make it down the hill, which was part of the fun. Brian and I would romp in the hill because we just didn't have it. My dad would go out there and play with us for a while. We had lots of friends in the neighborhood and they would all come up to use our hill. By late day you would see bunches of kids just on our hill in our yard. It was just a great time. We used to play football in the snow and my brother would let me play until I reached puberty. It was just boys and girls having fun. My stepmother would come out and join us. It would just be fun.

(Jacqueline Joyner)

121

I dated my senior year and it was kind of weird because all the boys I knew were my brother's friends. So I didn't start dating until Brian went to Syracuse and I stopped being Brian's younger sister. I had about three boyfriends that year. We would go over to his house or the movies and watch cable. I started to feel a little inferior with my social status because these boys were from wealthy parents. He had his own car. Money was no big deal. Some had huge houses. I experienced stuff I never got to experience like Sting. Jonathan opened my eyes to not being the norm. I dated rich guys at first. There was an airport near Fort Washington that Jonathan took me to. Jonathan had a Blazer and we would go there and watch planes and drink apple boy and listen to strange music, like Sting. I wasn't very good at sneaking out. Jonathan called me at about midnight. I never skipped class except on Senior Skip Day and I was so nervous. I ended up going to somebody else's school so on Senior Skip Day I didn't even take the day back. So Jonathan called and I didn't even know how to sneak out. I went out through the den door and he met me on the side. When I came back in I left the den light on. I left my shoes at the door—I left all my stuff at the door. It pretty much told [my dad] I was out. My dad wasn't too worried. They tease me to this day that they didn't worry about me sneaking out much because it was obvious I didn't do it on a regular basis.

(Jacqueline Joyner)

I wasn't aware of D.C. as the center of the free world. It probably seemed more unusual when we were younger because we would show off when people visited—especially [the] Air and Space Museum, the exhibit where you could make your own fighter plane. We went every day and by the end of the summer we would exhaust the possibilities of how to build it. We played soccer right on the Mall. We lived on the other side of the Mall, so we would just take

Standing prominently on Connecticut Avenue in the Cleveland Park neighborhood, the Uptown remains a thriving theater. (Courtesy Wymer Photo Collection, HSW Collections.)

a ten-minute walk. We knew kids everywhere didn't get to play soccer in front of important looking buildings or go to the museum every day.

(Danny Rose)

We played Street Theater and then the Putt Putt. We went to the movies a lot—the Avalon, the Jennifer, and the Uptown. Tenley was the big one, but now there is 4000 Wisconsin, which didn't come along until I was in college. I would invite eight people over to my house and we would have a movie festival and cook up a lot of microwave popcorn and watch movies. I would try to bring friends from different arenas to meet . . . It wasn't always such a good idea to mix friends from different places, but I didn't realize this until college. I could see how my interaction with friends was different depending on how I knew them.

(Cosby Hunt)

I don't remember doing much east of the park except for getting my hair cut on Georgia Avenue or getting my driver's license. Certainly I would go down to the Mall. The Air and Space Museum was just the greatest. I remember on the Mall there was a little playground that had a big dinosaur for kids to play on. It was huge, at least it seemed huge at the time. I don't remember what kind it was, but it was a four-legged rhinoceros looking one. I remember climbing on that and playing on a merry-go-round down near the African Art Museum.

(Cosby Hunt)

We used to play make believe all the time. My babysitters were teenagers who lived on my block, Rosie, Edwina, and Stacey. My friend Becky always wanted to play Snow White or Goldilocks and the Three Bears, and we'd have to act out the entire story. Our favorite toys were sit 'n spin, lemon twist, stilts, Simon, and the game Trouble. My problem was I could play a game over and over and over again. But Sit 'n Spin really took the cake. There's a disc that you put on the ground and there's a pole in the middle and then there's a smaller disc, which you twist yourself around. The bottom disc moves and you just get yourself extremely dizzy and fall over.

(Tracy Ferguson)

My brother and I still hang out. We had a lot of boys about the same age as us. We'd play outside—football, baseball, basketball—in our driveway. We didn't have to go very far because all the boys lived on the block. We maybe rode bikes down to the schoolyard. We had six or seven guys within a block and we always played outside. I can't remember Brady Bunch episodes like other people my age, because I was always outside playing. We would play at the schoolyard because it was in the neighborhood.

(Adam Vann)

We must have gone to the Smithsonian with school. But as soon as I found out there was a whole museum for planes and a whole museum for cars and trucks and stuff like that, I think that was about it. We would go once or twice a month because I wanted to see it all again. Nothing has changed. In fourth grade we discovered the Capital Children's Museum and that place was so great. That was the end all and be all. I'm sure even today I could go there and enjoy myself. It's built for kids to run around put firemen's suits on and slide down the poles and crawl in a simulated underground. It was such a great place. They had a big cooty outside. It was so

Tracy Ferguson and cousins Lori Dodson and Shari Fletcher jumping, 1977. (Courtesy Tracy Ferguson.)

cool and it is so unheralded, too. It is such a shame.

(Thaddeus Marcus Verhoff)

1981–82 was when I knew the music scene. I had a babysitter who came over and would play his records because his parents didn't like him playing them in the house. He had all the old D.C. bands like Minor Threat and The Teen Idols and a great bunch of music came in the house that way. That was the first time I associated music with D.C. I was probably five or six and it stuck with me ever since, going to free shows at Fort Reno out by Wilson there. It's just so great. It was nice to be introduced to music so early. This is music from kids who grew up where I did.

(Thaddeus Marcus Verhoff)

Skavacados was a Ska band that was most notable. It was a bunch of your friends together and everyone played. Everyone can be in it. You had a keyboard and a horn section and it was just the high-flying horns. It was great to be in a band with all those kids . . . We played at Maret a couple of times and then at Fort Reno . . . It was a thrill for me to play at Fort Reno even though there were like ten people there . . . That was probably the best band we played in and we wrote our own music and it wasn't as big as it is now. People came because they wanted to hear you play and dance to the music.

(Thaddeus Marcus Verhoff)

6. Remembering the Neighborhoods

We lived on 2002 Twelfth Street, NW, Twelfth and U. It was just turning over to colored around then. When I was young I can remember the white neighbors who lived across the street, the Barrys. Also, the Sellhausens were there. Up Twelfth Street there was a big farmhouse with a big yard around it, and Perry, who went to the North Pole, lived there and he had a little girl he called Snowbird. My brother Stanley used to play with her. There was white all up to V Street. That was after I was born until I was eight or nine years old . . . Evidently it was a pretty nice neighborhood for the African Americans. I could go around the block and there was a doctor on every corner on Thirteenth Street. Dr. Davis on Eleventh and U, Dr. Warfield at Eleventh and T—he was head of Freedman's Hospital. Then on T Street was Dr. Gaskin, the dentist, and then . . . up Thirteenth Street Dr. Curtis; he also had been a chief surgeon at the Freedman's Hospital. You'd go down U Street and you get Dr. Gray and the Pythian Temple. The Pythian Temple was made by a colored architect and is still there—the architect named Langford. I can remember when the neighborhood was mixed. We knew the Barrys and the Sellhausens. The Barrys lived right next door to us and the Sellhausens lived in front of us. They had a stationery store on Georgia Avenue. I can remember them. They finally moved and it became completely black.

(Helen Combs Wood)

At that time we were very satisfied with ourselves and the neighborhood. We had our own little theaters. We went to the Howard Theater and there was a movie theater on Eleventh Street, the Hiawatha. There was a little theater named the Dunbar where the Lincoln Theater is now. We used to go to the serials every week. *The Perils of Pauline* and *The Red Circle*, when the girl got ready to do something wrong there was a red circle and we used to all paint red circles on our hands. The movies were 5¢—the nickelodeon . . . Later when I went to Howard, they had something called The Supper Show. On Saturdays that was a big gathering place for the teenagers. They had stage acts along with a picture. I remember the acts later when I was grown.

(Helen Combs Wood)

Where the Carnegie [Library] is now, my mother used to take me to the park there at Seventh and New York Avenue right next to the library. I went to the Zoo, of course. I wasn't too much of a movie fan. When I was smaller my mother would go to the theaters and take me with her. That was downtown along Seventh Street. There were two or three theaters. She liked the movies. We went to the theater that caved in on Eighteenth and Columbia Road, the Knickerbocker. We went there a lot. It caved in years and years ago when so many people lost their lives.

(Dorothy Marita King)

My favorite candy store was Velati's candy store—the most delicious caramels on Earth. 40¢ a pound. Back then when money wasn't like it was today, we would go in and get a half of pound. They were on Ninth and G. They specialized in caramels. Velati's was the best.

(Dorothy Marita King)

Georgia Avenue was racially integrated and our next-door neighbors were white. Most of the other streets were occupied entirely by white families. There were some black families in the area of Sixth Street, NW and Howard University, and Girard Street, NW bordering on the Howard University campus.

(Frank R. Jackson)

As a teenager I went to the Howard Theater on T Street, NW near Seventh Street— the only bone fide vaudeville theater. Of course, the movies were widely patronized by youngsters. If you got there say before 5:30 you could get in for something like 10 or 15¢. That rate for the

Helen Combs Wood grew up around Twelfth and T Streets, NW along the same block as Duke Ellington's family house. (Courtesy Wymer Photo Collection, HSW Collections.)

Frank Jackson played in the playgrounds of Howard University. (Courtesy Wymer Photo Collection, HSW Collections.)

The Lincoln Theater on Twelfth and U Streets, NW in the heart of the Shaw neighborhood. The Lincoln had both a movie screen and an adjacent ballroom called the Lincoln Colonnade. (Courtesy Wymer Photo Collection, HSW Collections.)

127

earlier timed movies was a policy at all the theaters. You could get in for a few pennies if you got there early. Now there was the Lincoln on U Street and further up there was the Republic. Up near Fifteenth on U Street there was the Booker T.

(Frank R. Jackson)

The playgrounds were too far away to play and my mother wanted us to be under her watchful eye. Now there were a lot of vacant lots. For example we lived between Fifteenth and Sixteenth on T and between Fourteenth and Fifteenth on T, there were no apartments built at that time, so that was a vacant lot. Between Fifteenth and Sixteenth on U there were no buildings so that was another vacant lot. We would go particularly to the one on Sixteenth Street and pick the clovers and tie them together to make garlands, necklaces, and so forth. The boys, of course, took advantage of those vacant lots to play ball.

(Marion Jackson Pryde)

Southwest was a mixed neighborhood. I was almost a member of the Edward League, the Methodist Church organization down the street because several of my friends went there. I used to play around with them and go to their meetings on Sunday evenings. I was considered almost a member. My parents sort of looked over that kind of thing. They weren't that strict and they believed you didn't treat anyone any different. That's the kind of neighborhood I grew up in. The people next door to us were Catholic and I remember a [Catholic] family on the corner, but many people were not Catholic. It was racially mixed as well. Across the street there were black families and over on E Street. There were also Italian families and we lived on Tenth Street where there

were two alleys—Golden and Liberty—and there were dwellings in those places. Blacks lived there.

(Joseph Eugene Zeis)

There was a theater in Southwest Washington and we used to call it "the Dump," but I don't remember its formal name. How it got the name "the Dump," I'll never know, but it was a popular neighborhood spot. This was the days of the silent movies and somebody played the piano. The theater was owned by two maiden ladies; Sadie Cohen was one of them. She'd come up and down the aisle and on Saturdays it was mostly kids. We'd be excited and talking and she'd march down the aisles saying, "Be quiet. You kids be quiet. Now cut that out." Maybe it was the Ashleigh Theater on Seventh and E Streets, SW.

(Joseph Eugene Zeis)

January 1922 was the night when the Knickerbocker Theater roof collapsed, and I think 100 people died there on Eighteenth and Columbia Road. The snow started falling Friday afternoon and [fell] all through the night. Saturday my sister and I couldn't go to the movies at the Circle Theater because there was so much snow. I remember staring out the window at my father's shop waiting for the snow to reach a bar in front of the house at the sidewalk. We were waiting for the snow to cover that bar 36 inches off the ground, and late that night, around 9 o'clock, was when the roof collapsed at the Knickerbocker Theater. By 10 o'clock there were many, many ambulances zooming down Seventeenth Street to the old emergency hospital. After several of them clanged down the street, my father wanted to find out what was going on, so he cut a path from his shop to

Joseph and Rosemary Zeis, c. 1917. (Courtesy Joseph Eugene Zeis.)

the streetcar tracks, which were clear. He walked out there and one of the ambulances stopped as the ambulance reached the corner of Pennsylvania Avenue and he asked the driver what the problem was and he was told then. There was no radio or telephone back then.

(Markus Ring)

My father ended up buying a grocery store in an area which was country—Tenleytown. Connecticut Avenue was developed to Chevy Chase, but Wisconsin Avenue and River Road, that was Tenleytown, and that was where the commercial areas were. The grocery store was around the 4900 block of Wisconsin Avenue at Forty-second Street

George and Marvin Tievsky in front of the family car in Tenleytown, c. 1934. (Courtesy Marvin Tievsky.)

school in Tenleytown. As a matter of fact they had just built the Janney School on Albemarle Street. Prior to that we had an older red brick country-type school with less than a half dozen rooms in it. It went through the third grade until they put an addition on the Janney School. [The old red brick school] was sold to the church next door. Crossing past the Janney School where Hechinger's was, there was a blacksmith shop and his daughters went to school with us. Watching him make horseshoes was fascinating. We still had horses. There was ice and not many people had refrigerators. The grocery store itself was refrigerated with blocks of ice. Eventually my father turned it into a liquor store after the repeal of Prohibition. Park Liquor was the name of the store. Our grocery store was called Wisconsin Market and then Wisconsin Market and Liquor Store.

(Marvin Tievsky)

where a gift shop is now. Growing up my brother and I worked in the store. We worked there after school and my mother worked there, too. We lived above the store, too. It has changed so much. Washington was a small city. We lived out in the country and that was fun. Nobody ever locked their doors. We had no air conditioning and we had windows open with flypaper everywhere and fly swatters. The city was very clean. We used to have hydrant trucks come about 12 o'clock every night and wash the streets down in the entire city. We had street sweepers that swept the street every day.

(Marvin Tievsky)

First in Northeast we went to the Blow School for four years and then we went to

There were houses up and down Wisconsin Avenue by then. Wisconsin was a two-lane street. Wisconsin had houses but no office buildings until the 1960s. On the left-hand side was a two-lane road and the right-hand side had streetcars that ran from downtown to Bethesda. Streetcars ran from downtown to Baltimore and Annapolis. Those ran two at a time. We had open streetcars with straw seats in the summertime. In Tenleytown many of the streets were not cut through and American University Park was just three small buildings and many vacant lots. I was at AU [American University] the other day and now it is quite a complex.

(Marvin Tievsky)

The main shopping street was F Street, and Seventh Street had the department stores: Hecht's, Lansburgh's, and Kann's. There were all kinds of shops and clothing stores on F Street. Downtown was very active. To go to the movies we went to Connecticut Avenue to the Avalon. The recreation was really tight. In downtown you ran into everyone you knew because all the big movie houses were there. A place like the Avalon would get second runs. Theaters had acts in between movies like clowns, comedies, acrobats, and big bands. Today, [the old movie palaces] would be under historic preservation. Some movie palaces brought in big bands like Cab Calloway and Duke Ellington. Later on, when air conditioning came in, we used to go to the movies to cool off.

(Marvin Tievsky)

The shopping district of Washington in the 1920s and '30s was clearly identified with F and G Streets and Seventh and Eighth Streets, NW. In my experiences as a boy, I could do all my Christmas shopping on a total budget of less than $2, making use of Woolworth's and Kresge's on G Street, and the Palais Royale, across the street from Woodward & Lothrop's.

(Austin Kiplinger)

Our house was at 1121 Harvard Street, across from Wilson Normal Teachers College, later incorporated into the University of the District of Columbia. I went to kindergarten there in an experimental class handled by teachers in training. Down the street at the corner of Eleventh was a Sanitary Grocery Store.

(Austin Kiplinger)

I was born in Northeast but moved to Friendship Heights. It was like the country

Downtown on Seventh Street, NW. (Courtesy Wymer Photo Collection, HSW Collections.)

Austin Kiplinger pushing his wagon as his grandmother Cora Miller Kiplinger looks on in front of his home at 1121 Harvard Street, NW, c. 1922. (Courtesy Kiplinger Archives.)

then. You could hear roosters in the morning. We had apple trees and would climb them. It was rural back then or at least undeveloped . . . 5327 Belt Road, NW off of Military Road. I think they bought it for $6,000 . . . When it rained we'd put on bathing suits and play in the alley. We'd climb up apple trees together— simple pleasures in those days. When the iceman came you'd put a card with how many pounds you wanted. We had an icebox and they'd bring it in. You'd have a card with numbers and you put the number up on the card. They had a horse and buggy, but there were some on a truck. We'd always try to get pieces of ice from the truck and when it melted we needed to go to the store.

(Janet Kasdon Lobred)

When I went to Georgetown it was divided. There were some poor people in Georgetown and we used to collect food to bring to the people across the street. It was racially mixed back then. It was interesting. I liked that—going to different areas and being around different people. Now Friendship Heights is the middle of the city, but growing up it was like the suburbs. In Georgetown people were poor or rich. I had a friend from Western who was Greek and whose father owned a delicatessen.

(Janet Kasdon Lobred)

I have very fond memories of going with Mother down to Fourteenth and Park Road, which was sort of the center. We would pass the Sacred Heart Church on Sixteenth and Park. At that time you could walk on their stone wall and I remember being so excited to walk on the wall when we got to Sixteenth Street . . . I remember walking up Park Road and along the wall and going up to Fourteenth and Park Road. Park Road

The People's Drug Store sitting prominently at the corner of Fourteenth and Park Roads in the heart of Columbia Heights. (Courtesy Wymer Photo Collection, HSW Collections.)

was very exciting in those days. On one corner was this beautiful, massive, big Riggs bank. On another corner was a People's Drug Store with a counter where you could get sodas and food. It was very, very special. I remember eating grilled cheese sandwiches there. Also, on the third corner, across Fourteenth Street, was the Tivoli Theater. That was the height of beauty and excitement. I remember seeing *Ben Hur* there and seeing it many, many times until my father came and got us because movies would play over and over back then. There was another movie house about a block and a half down called the Savoy Theater. It was a lower-class theater and wasn't nearly as attractive, but for 10¢ you could go there and see all kinds of funny little ten-minute movies and it was an open-air theater in the back. Other things that I remember along that area was a wonderful Arcade Market. The Arcade Market was a wonderful closed market with all kinds of stands. I remember

the fish stand; my mother was always buying Spanish mackerel. I remember the sweets and the bakery and they would offer me a cookie, but I didn't like sweets. But when we got to the deli counter I would always ask for an olive—I adored olives. The whole market was interesting with flowers and just excitement.

(Flora Blumenthal Atkin)

It was a working-class neighborhood. My father was a streetcar conductor on a streetcar line right behind me. No women on my block worked. There were lots of Italian families and lots of Irish Catholic working-class families. I remember playing with the kids in the neighborhood. We did things like sit on the corner and watch streetcars go by and trying to identify automobiles. They were so rare in those days. No one on my block had one . . . We played games like kick the can and hide 'n go seek and others in the alley. I was

Frolicking in front of the fountains at the Library of Congress, 1921. (Courtesy Robert H. McNeill.)

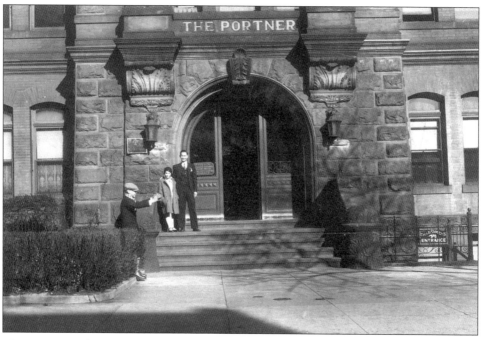

Florence Crawford Marvil and her father on the steps of the Portner Apartments located at Fifteenth and V Streets, NW, c. 1932. (Courtesy Florence Crawford Marvil.)

between three and four when we played outside with the kids in the neighborhood. My house had about 12 steps down to the alley . . . Behind the alley was the railroad tracks and then a big open field. It was like a playground for us although it was full of rocks and grass and bottles. After school and on the weekends we were much more likely to play in the alley than out front. Out front they did at night when the alley was darker. Older kids shoot craps and younger kids play games, but in the alley it was fun. We'd play games. There were many places to play hide and seek. We built fires in the open space and made potatoes . . . My best friend was a boy named Raymond Britton and I liked being friends with him because he was an only child and his mother and father lived on the other side of town. His grandmother raised him and his grandfather was a

railroad engineer. They had the nicest house on the block. I think part of my appeal to him was I got invited to lunch and he had things my family didn't have.

(Richard E. Hawes)

I lived at the Portner Apartment in downtown on Fifteenth Street between U and V Streets. It was the second oldest building in the city. We had huge apartments. Our apartment had four bedrooms. There was a private dining room for residents and tennis courts on the roof. We lived there for 18 years before it shut down and became the Dunbar Hotel.

(Florence Crawford Marvil)

We lived in Georgetown, which seems rather unusual. At that time it was a predominantly black, family centered neighborhood. We didn't realize all the prejudices. We had a playground and wonderful teachers and good schools. We had wonderful times through high school. Life was enjoyable for us and we didn't have worries. We didn't know we were poor or missing anything because we had fun. We knew all the neighbors. We sat out front, chatted and talked, and went to school or work. Everybody looked after everybody else's children and if someone spoke to you, you paid attention, and there was a

price to pay if you didn't pay attention. I had chores in my house that I had to do. My parents worked and by the time I was done with my school activities, did my chores—I was responsible for washing clothes—and did my homework, I was ready to go to sleep. In those times your day was full. In the summers you had more time.

(Clara Sharon Taylor)

On Fessenden Street in Northwest Washington stands a small white house, a bungalow, which was very popular in the 1920s. It was built generally of one story, sometimes with a kind of half second story, with the front door opening into the living room, and, as usual with houses of this period, very few closets. Kitchens were built with four walls and a sink. The householder was responsible for buying all appliances—there weren't many—and cabinets for storage. This was the first house I knew. There are two houses built there now but in 1920 between our house and Wisconsin Avenue there were only fields. There was a very large field behind our house, which was owned by a Mr. Markham, who, to the delight of a five year old, owned a horse. One sunny afternoon the horse got loose, ran into the area beside our house and galloped happily around with my father and Mr. Markham in hot pursuit, a chase in which I would have been glad to join if my scaredy-cat parents would have allowed me.

(Jo Forbes Carpenter)

Jo Forbes Carpenter in Tenleytown, 1928. (Courtesy Jo Forbes Carpenter.)

Only three blocks from our house was Western Avenue, the boundary between D.C. and Maryland. River Road was then a bumpy country lane, so little traveled that in 1939 when my father taught me to drive, he took me that way as being the safest

Woodward & Lothrop, the downtown shopping destination for many Washingtonians. (Courtesy Wymer Photo Collection, HSW Collections.)

with the least traffic . . . There were a number of farms and small houses along it, one with a hand-scrawled sign in front that said, "Fresh egg for sale." We always wondered why nobody bought that egg.

(Jo Forbes Carpenter)

Going downtown meant using the trolley, a noisy, rattling green and brown vehicle, which employed the service of two men, a driver and a conductor. Some of these trolleys had an entrance at the side, but on most of them one entered at the back where one paid one's fare, leaving the driver to do nothing but drive—probably a very sensible arrangement . . . From Friendship Heights into downtown Washington the cars were powered by overhead electric wires until they reached Georgetown, at which point all the children

on board would rush to the back to see the changeover made to underground power. Two or three men would emerge from an underground lair directly beneath the tracks to take down the trolley pole, which caused the lights to go out and a surprisingly sudden silence to occur—a silence which was broken by a shattering rattle as the driver released the emergency brake. I always wanted to see this underground den, an entertainment I never enjoyed, but a cousin who worked for Capital Transit told me it was a real little apartment, complete with kitchen and bathroom.

(Jo Forbes Carpenter)

Shopping downtown meant Woodward & Lothrop, and until some time in the '30s, the North Building was owned by a

137

different company and called the Palais Royale. "Woody's Balcony" at the G Street entrance was the place for meeting ones friends. It was also a nice place to watch the activity below, never any male shoppers but ladies always wearing hats and gloves. In fact, everybody wore hats whenever they stepped outside their front doors . . . At some point on F or G Street there was a furrier which had the figure of an enormous white bear in front of its door; "At the sign of the big white bear," as their advertisement went. As time went on this bear became dirtier and shabbier and Arthur Godfrey on his morning radio program made so much fun of it, it was finally removed.

(Jo Forbes Carpenter)

I remember the house had iron steps. This house had been occupied by Mr. Al Jolson's father, [Moses Yoelson]. My father was a shochet. According to the Jewish religion, poultry and other animals are slaughtered in a certain way. He was performing this type of work in Cheyenne. He heard Al Jolson's father was going to retire so we moved. We didn't have electricity. Just gas jets. Most of the animals are slaughtered somewhere else now. People would either purchase the chicken from him or bring the chickens to be slaughtered. It cost 15¢ to slaughter the chicken and then the feathers had to be plucked. Either my mother or they'd hire somebody to pick feathers. He also performed circumcisions . . . The rent on the house in Southwest was $40 a month. The little groceries, most families that owned them lived above the stores. Our house was like a regular house on Four and a Half Street. Most of the other houses were businesses. I guess [there was] no zoning like today. There was a variety store,

a dry goods store, and a hardware store. There were some Chinese laundries.

(Larry Rosen)

Sidewalks were like brick. To the left of my house was Sam's Barber Shop and we got cuts for 35¢. I had a friend who was a tinner and later had a shoe store. The fighter Joe Louis was popular. There was a liquor store across the street and they set up a radio on the nights of the fight and everyone would crowd around and listen to the fight. The beginning of the block was called Four and a Half Street. There was a streetcar running up and down and then a bus. You'd buy a pass for $1 and it would last all week. People were friendly. You never heard of robberies. If people got drunk, a policeman would take him and order a patrol wagon. I do faintly recall horse troughs because cars were just coming on. I went to the Old Jefferson on Sixth Street and later it moved to Seventh Street. I went to Central High in Northwest, which later became Cardozo. I graduated from Central in '41 and in '59 I bought this drugstore, Smith Pharmacy, that was two blocks away from where I attended high school.

(Larry Rosen)

I'd occasionally go downtown for the movies. The Capitol Theater for a stage show. We went for a big show but not that often. There were a number of theaters downtown like the Keith's. One of the nicest old movie houses was called "the Little" down on Ninth Street, just below where the library is now. That specialized in what they today call art films and it had a lot of British films. Occasionally we would go to the Newsreel Theater, which was located between H and New York Avenue. It is in that triangle there and is a beautiful art deco building

Boys playing around Fort Totten Park. (Courtesy Wymer Photo Collection, HSW Collections.)

built specially for that, and all it did was show newsreels.

(Myles MacCrimmon Johnson)

I lived at 56 Crittenden Street, NE, a neighborhood of row houses built in the late '30s. A lot of the neighbors were coming back from the war and were in a strictly middle-class neighborhood, with a lot of men just starting out . . . The woods where we played were right in back of our houses from Fort Totten and North Capitol to the firehouse. It had poison ivy but we would run there anyway. The big woods was across the street, called Fort Totten. Our parents didn't want us in the big woods because we could get lost easily. We used to jump on the rocks, but the rocks weren't really rocks, but old gateposts that had been placed around the wall near Constitution Avenue for storage. We used

to jump from one to the other. They were like cemetery stones and we jumped on them and played games on them. We would throw rocks down the ravine and board games and do what kids did.

(Sandy Berk)

The things in the city that I remember are Rock Creek Park. I must have spent a lot of time in Rock Creek Park as a child. I remember when there were ducks and fords instead of bridges. I remember when the park would be closed because the fords were flooded and the car couldn't navigate it. I remember when we had to stop to let the ducks cross the road.

(Sally Lichtenstein Berk)

Growing up in Northwest was quiet—not very exciting, but pleasant. We used to go sledding in the winter on Appleton Street.

There used to be more snow on that street than almost anywhere else in town. In winter it was a steep hill and there is something about the geography of the place that kept the snow from melting, and it was hot in the summer . . . I remember when they first put in the sidewalks, because when I first moved in there were no sidewalks. This was when I was five or six and then they planted maples when I was seven and they are big now.

(Alison Luchs)

Westover Drive was a hill and our house was on the top of the hill and it had three stories so when we went to the top story, which was my sister's bedroom, to watch the fireworks; we could see the Capitol and the Washington Monument, especially in the winter. We could see the buildings and the monuments. There we were on our hill looking out at this beautiful expanse of grand buildings.

(Judy Scott Feldman)

Sally Lichtenstein Berk with her father, Harold Lichtenstein, at Bolling Air Force Base, 1947. (Courtesy Sally Lichtenstein Berk.)

Judy Scott Feldman grew up on Westover Drive in Southeast Washington. (Courtesy Wymer Photo Collection, HSW Collections.)

It was a wonderful neighborhood full of kids. Another thing about that neighborhood was the architecture was interesting because the houses were trap houses. They were all built in the '20s and '30s and were all different. Our house was this big stone house with these sparkling stones in it and a slate roof. When pieces from the roof fell off, we would have something to play hopscotch with. Our neighbors had a split timber. All the houses were different. They were full of kids. Our next-door neighbors had five kids and the neighbors next to them had five kids. There were lots and lots of kids and we all played together right there because there was no traffic because it was off of Pennsylvania Avenue and a circle. We used to play softball, baseball, kickball in the middle of the street. Someone would scream "car" and we would have to get out of the street. The only thing we had to be careful of was Mrs. Curtis's pink vase. She had a four-foot-high pink vase sitting on her stoop. We couldn't hit it.

(Judy Scott Feldman)

We moved in the early '70s when I started going to school. We moved into a housing area called Park Naylor Apartments—a big apartment area with several acres. It is cut off from everything around it and like a neighborhood in a neighborhood, just without the streets. This is in Southeast off the 2500 block of Naylor Road. It's a cool little area. It's nice.

(Keith Lofton)

141

Danny Rose's class photo from Peabody Elementary School, Ms. Wilkins's class of 1977–1978. (Courtesy Danny Rose.)

Fort Dupont was a place that I used to frequent during the summers for picnics and family outings and Frisbee and concerts and kid's games and football . . . So much good music filtered through that area because it's an area of free music and an area that's conducive for people who live on that side of town to cook out and barbecue, and it just extends the culture that goes on in that part of town.

(Keith Lofton)

Capitol Hill was a special place in the '70s. There were plenty of children to spend time with and play touch football with in the alley. I had this nice group of friends that stayed together a long time, even after everyone dispersed to different schools. When we were in elementary school, we were all together. The public schools were

still good and a lot of white middle-class parents were very committed to public education—more than today. But by junior high everyone had moved away or gone to private school.

(Danny Rose)

The great thing about the Hawthorn neighborhood is there were a lot of kids, so we would ride around the neighborhood on bikes. The streets were pretty quiet. Eric and Sandy lived very close to Lafayette so I usually had to ride a couple of miles to go over to their place. But I had friends in my neighborhood to run around with. We played a lot of hide and seek and dodge ball in people's yards and the moms and the dads kept the Kool-aid flowing. There were some woods right where Beech Street and Thirty-second Street intersect. I spent a lot

142

of time in those woods throwing rocks with my friends and getting into all sorts of mayhem in the woods. There was a lot to do for kids in the woods and with friends.

(Cosby Hunt)

I used to love Georgetown. In sixth grade we used to walk from school. We used to walk and window shop. Of course, we only had about $10 so we could only buy the earrings from the vendors, but it was fun to just walk around and get the flavor of the area. I think Washington has lost some of that flavor. I sound like my grandmother sounded, I'm sure. If you go during the day at 1 o'clock on a Monday, you could still feel that. If you go on a weekend evening, it seems like Georgetown is trying to be a little entertainment center and it loses some of its character. I love the little houses and the people. I enjoyed seeing familiar faces as I walked down the street. I would know a classmate or a classmate's parents. It was definitely a community atmosphere and seemed quite quaint. Now it just seems very commercial, especially on the weekends.

(Tracy Ferguson)

Reading comic books in front of the Windsor Apartments at 1425 T Street, NW, 1939. (Courtesy Album #12, HSW Collections.)

7. Working around Washington

When I went to high school, I used to write out the menus for a dining room on Thirteenth and Wallach Streets, NW. I used to do some clerical work for the manager.

(Dorothy Marita King)

Walter Johnson of the Washington Senators at Griffith Stadium, 1916. (Courtesy Richard Mansfield Collection, HSW Collections.)

There was always some sort of a job available. From the time I was 14 for a few years, I worked at Griffith Stadium selling peanuts, hot dogs, and things on the stands. We were supposed to be moving and not watching, and getting rid of peanuts and cracker jacks. I didn't have a chance to meet players, but I knew them very well and had seen some of the greatest ball players perform in that setting: Walter Johnson, Babe Ruth, Ty Cobb, and managers like Bucky Harris. I saw the 1924 World Series because I worked there.

(Frank R. Jackson)

When I was younger there was a small church on Thirteenth Street called Trinity Baptist and I played for one of the afternoon services there. They paid me about 50¢ a Sunday or something like that. You had a lot of things to do when you were part of a family. You had the washing and the ironing and cleaning up the house, and the boys, in addition to going to school, had odd jobs. My brother sold newspapers and he would take my younger sister Ursula and put her on the wagon with the papers. He loved to take her because he said people seeing her there would buy more papers from him. Everybody contributed what they could to the family budget. The girls contributed in the house but not really working outside like the boys.

(Marion Jackson Pryde)

I was pretty good at algebra. Bookkeeping was my thing. I worked in the bank in high school at the school bank. We learned how to keep the books and make change and then of course we'd send it to another bank in the city. Our bank instructor was Helen Atwater. She was in charge of the bank. But we got some good experience.

(Robert Israel Silverman)

There was a fish market. Many had stores on Water Street on the waterfront. I didn't fish, but I helped out down there. My mother helped out down there on Friday, which was a busy fish day. I helped jump

deliveries. They served fish to various small retail stores around the community. These orders would be phoned in, so I helped deliver them. The driving guy was the son of the owner David Fones, and we'd deliver from one little grocery store to the next. We'd go as far as Silver Spring in those days. I made 25¢. I was just a kid, 13 or 14. I'd jump out and deliver the fish. This was 5 o'clock in the morning before school, but only on Fridays. We started school at 9 o'clock in those days—none of this 7:30 or 8 o'clock. I recall a lot of names of merchants along the fish line. They were all fish market establishments. I did this for three years. My mom was cashier and took orders as well.

(Joseph Eugene Zeis)

I worked down at the old Central Market on Seventh Street and Pennsylvania Avenue, NW for about a year and a half for Mrs. Cora

The Southwest waterfront in the 1940s. (Courtesy Wymer Photo Collection, HSW Collections.)

Markus Ring sitting on his wagon, 1926. (Courtesy Markus Ring.)

would stand on the streetcar platform in front of what is now the Renwick Gallery. The streetcar driver would let us in the front door. Then we would walk down the aisle selling the newspapers. The papers were 2¢ and people would give us a nickel and say keep the change. The driver would crawl at the lowest speed from Seventeenth up to Eighteenth giving us time to sell our papers because we had to get off at the next stop.

(Markus Ring)

When I was in the 11th and 12th grades, my father lived in the Dupont Circle Apartments, and I attended Western High School. There I edited *The Breeze*, the student newspaper. This job had the advantage of giving me license to go practically anywhere in my editorial capacity, and I used it with glee.

(Austin Kiplinger)

Ridgeway who had a bakery stand and who employed me on Saturday while I was in Tech High School. I worked from six in the morning to 7 o'clock at night. I made $5, which was pretty good at the time, and one doughnut down at the bakery store. We sold bakery goods. I was one of the clerks. I shelled out bread, rolls, pastry, you name it. I also washed and stored the pans. This was where the Archives stands today.

(Markus Ring)

Back in the '20s there were seven papers: the *Post*, the *Star*, the *News*, the *Times*, the *Herald*, the *Bulletin*, and I think, *Sporting News*. The fellow who printed them would give us ten copies of the latest and we

I was a camp counselor for two years in my late teens at a camp in Pennsylvania and I had a wonderful time. It was a coed camp so I had a wonderful time. I was a junior counselor at first and then was asked to come back. I did a lot of stuff with dance there.

(Flora Blumenthal Atkin)

During high school I worked on Saturdays and after school at Magruder's grocery store downtown near the Mayflower. At that time it was a prestigious grocery store. I was 16 and had to go to the Franklin School to get an underaged working permit. I used to fill grocery orders for rich people on Massachusetts Avenue and a few boys would deliver them. No girls had those jobs.

(Richard E. Hawes)

I went to Central High in Northwest. I graduated in '41. I was assistant sports editor my last year. That was a big thing. I liked sports. In high school I helped my dad. Sometimes during the holidays I'd be the cashier in the market. No cash register, just the money in the cash box.

(Larry Rosen)

When I was 16 I taught Sunday school to a group of fifth grade boys, which was challenging. I still see them today and they still remember me as Miss Sharon. I taught the Endeavor Society at about 15 years old because the person who was in charge got sick. I had younger children who were seven and eight, and not those fifth grade boys with some of them as large as I was. I was the First Baptist Church Sunday school teacher; I sang in the choir and I was the junior superintendent of the Christian Endeavor Society. We participated in so

Flora Blumenthal Atkin en pointe, c. 1927. (Courtesy Flora Blumenthal Atkin.)

Sharon Clara Taylor taught classes at the First Baptist Church of Georgetown. (Courtesy Wymer Photo Collection, HSW Collections.)

much and we knew what we wanted to do. Back then most of us who came through school just thought of teaching elementary school. By 11th grade I knew that unless I could get a scholarship, I was not going to college because there was no money. I guess at the end of World War II things were getting harder and people needed employees. By the middle of 12th grade I went to work as a clerk in the Surgeon General's Office from about 3 to 7 p.m., so they let us out of school at 2:30. At that time the office was on 1717 E Street where the World Bank is now. We filed and read papers. By May, the Civil Service Commission came through the schools and permitted us to take the examinations. I worked in Scientific Research and Development as a messenger and then a clerk's job when others went to college.

(Clara Sharon Taylor)

I started working for people when I was 6 or 7. I would carry people's errands and would bring the money to my family. I would take from Fourth Street to Fourteenth Street and W with laundry. I went by the cows and the dairy. I was an errand girl, and I would go to the store for the elderly. Mama would not allow us to take money from the elderly.

(Loretta Carter Hanes)

World War II, there were blackouts and rations. It was a scary time and a hard time. There were air raids. We put the light on and the warden would find you if you were in violation. I was in high school and took a job at the water department. I was in the clerical department. It was hard because I would get home in the middle of the night. It was not comfortable for me because it was segregated still.

(Loretta Carter Hanes)

Loretta Carter Hanes and friends Daisy, Dorothy, and Thelma at Armstrong High, 1943. (Courtesy Loretta Carter Hanes.)

Charlie Brotman smiling for the camera in Rock Creek Park, c. 1939. (Courtesy Charlie Brotman.)

We lived on Fourth and Todd Place, NE. It was a one-block street with row houses. 1918 Fourth Street, NE was Mother's Market and we lived there—my sister, me, my mom, and my dad lived behind the store in a storeroom. We were open seven days. My sister was five years older and we worked in the store bagging potatoes and waiting on customers.

(Charles Brotman)

My life changed when I went to St. Albans. I think maybe because my best friend was in the class and I wanted to stay. I became an eager beaver. Not my first year, but from my second on and I ended up number two in my class. I began to desire to achieve. My best friend at that time was E. Barrett Prettyman Jr. He has been working for $1 a year to investigate the D.C. government recently and Eric was my best friend. The courthouse where the Starr investigations went on was the E. Barrett Prettyman Courthouse—that was his father. As a matter of fact my first business venture was the P&F Shoeshine Company. Actually we got a full-page write-up by the *Washington Star* about our shoeshine company. We used our bikes and covered a pretty wide area.

(George Ferris Jr.)

I was a waiter with roller skates at the Hot Shoppes in Rosslyn. You'd dine outside and skaters would go and take the orders. I also worked as a bus boy at National Airport. I worked at Safeway as a grocery clerk stocking shelves. Another odd job I had was working for a guy that had a magazine that promoted city events. It was a little advertising booklet that he put in taxicabs. So I went to the taxicab station and inserted the little holders in the taxicabs and stocked them. That was kind of a summer deal. I also worked as a stock boy in a warehouse doing inventory at the Hecht Company.

(Myles MacCrimmon Johnson)

[During World War II] there seemed to be a lot of activity right around Dupont Circle, because diagonally across from the Heurich House, on the same block, there was an officer's club. That was an interesting place for us to hang around. There were a lot of service personnel and music playing, and a lot was going on . . . I was 9 to 11 then. Because there were so many people around Dupont Circle, a number of us shined shoes to make some money. We'd just roller skate around the Circle and ask if the fellow wanted a shoeshine. We charged a quarter, hoping we would get a little bit of a tip, a nickel or a dime or a quarter if we were lucky. I found out very quickly that I wasn't very good at shining shoes . . . so I didn't make very much money.

(Damon Cordom)

I worked in Pittles Bakery for three years on weekends and some week nights. I was the only one in my immediate crowd who worked during high school. Pittles was on Nebraska and Connecticut Avenues. Since the bakery was two blocks from my house, I didn't lose much time commuting. I lost weight while I worked there which was surprising because I had access to sweets while I was there—as long as the customers didn't see me eating. I was pretty active and I had a horrendous dental bill because of eating there. My parents refused to pay it saying I was working.

(Damon Cordom)

I had paper routes in Congress Heights and I delivered the *Daily News* at Bolling Air Force Base. The paper route was a real

George Ferris Jr. as a toddler, 1929. (Courtesy George Ferris Jr.)

disaster, because you didn't make any money. The *Daily News* was only six days a week so I was happy about that. I did it for three years when I was in junior high. I was never without a paper route in that time.

(Tom Reese)

I think I needed a work permit from a downtown school to be working. This was in the summer. I learned to type at a really early age, I think because my father was a writer and we had typewriters around the house. First with the two fingers and then I

150

Congress Heights Class 6B, 1945. (Courtesy Tom Reese.)

took a typing class where you learned it officially. At one point in high school they told us we needed to learn shorthand too in case I needed to support myself. So I took a shorthand class in summer school and I enjoyed it. I always had summer jobs through high school and college. They all had secretarial duties but I was sometimes an editorial assistant. I had a lot of control over my paycheck. I remember it was exciting to make $1–2 an hour. It was big stuff.

(Susan Tassler Ginsberg)

Between the ages of seven and ten down around Union Station on Third Street, NE some of the fellows and I would make music and dance for people, and they would give us pennies, nickels, and dimes. When we didn't get money from that,

we would collect soda bottles and could return the bottles for a penny, a nickel, or a dime. Milk bottles got you a quarter. That's how you got the money to go to the movies.

(James Davis)

I ran a lawn service business in the summers starting in ninth grade. On the weekends I would do two or three lawns and sometimes during the week. I made some money and I had another guy working for me. It was terrible work and hard work. After that I vowed never to do another lawn. I am not one of those who likes to mow. My brother worked at an electronics store. My last year in high school and first two years in college I was a small appliance salesman.

(Sandy Berk)

151

James Davis in a studio photo, c. 1949. (Courtesy James Davis.)

My senior year in high school I worked as a stock clerk in a woman's wear store on Connecticut Avenue. It was fun to see how the store operated. There was an upstairs for organizing the clothes. It was probably assumed everyone was going to college and your parents made provisions for that, so there was not so much emphasis on working. Only after graduating were you interested in making a bit more money.

(Gretchen Roberts-Shorter)

I was the paperboy for the *Post*. Well, the *Evening Star* used to be the other paper. They were rivals. The circulation was probably split about half and half. The route started with my oldest brother, then was passed to me and my twin brother, and then we passed it along to our younger brother, so it was in our family for the longest time. I just remember getting up on this cold Sunday morning and for the Sunday paper you had to get up really early like 4 o'clock. They would get dropped off and this big mound of papers would be on our sidewalk corner . . . So you would go through and unwrap it and put it in paper bags, and you would go through your route and it was cold—though the stars were beautiful back then.

(Timothy Burton)

As a teenager I started working for Burton Nurseries. All the boys did, and we didn't go into management. We were in the crew. My dad and my uncle were probably particularly hard on us, because they didn't want the other workers to think we were given any special privileges, so we were worked to the bone. Actually I don't regret that experience because it instilled a sense of discipline and work ethic. I am quite happy to have gone through that.

(Timothy Burton)

My sisters and I were candy stripers and then during the school year, I also worked for the American Red Cross Leadership Council. I started in the seventh or eighth grade. We attended meetings downtown at the American Red Cross District of Columbia Headquarters and we organized a lot of the projects like filling gift boxes for people in institutions. The items were collected by the various charitable drives and organizations and we would put them in boxes and organize them. We were basically representing our schools. I was secretary and then vice president . . . One time they held a leadership training conference and they brought all of us to a college campus in Pennsylvania. We had workshops in managing people and leadership. I was in the eighth grade then and it was the first time I had ever gone anywhere by myself. The generation in which I grew up was the beginning of integration and my sister and I were in many instances of "firsts." I think I was the first black student who went to that black leadership training conference from Washington, for example. You always had to be circumspect, smart, and all of those things, because you were representing not only yourself but your family and your race, too.

(Breena Clarke Cooper)

My first job was at 14 and I worked as a supply clerk at the armory—the National Guard Armory. That was Marion Barry's job program and that was back when he was good. That was my first job and after that I did typical teenage jobs: a record store, a deli, this and that.

(Desmond Leary)

My summers were with my dad and I didn't even know that it would prepare me for

Breena Clarke stands by the family Chrysler, 1958. (Courtesy Breena Clarke.)

jobs and even what I do now. My dad loved his job and that's where he was, so pretty much to spend time with him that's what you did. That's where the bulk of his time went, so that's what you did. My dad is an attorney. I went to work with him every day during the summer when I was 13. There was one office on Fourteenth Street, NW near K Street. We would go in and he would go to his office and I would do clerical work. He would pay me in food, which was fine by me. As payment I would get to go to McDonald's. The funny thing is that gave me all my clerical experience.

(Jacqueline Joyner)

I worked at the St. Albans Tennis Club maintaining the courts, signing people up, and selling tennis balls. It was really a low-key job. I also had a job at the Metro Video

Connection, which is now where Politics and Prose is. I played in local tennis tournaments so I got a ranking in D.C. in singles and doubles. My partner from high school, Ed Miller, and I ranked number one in D.C. for doubles for a few years, so summers also involved planning some tennis tournaments.

(Cosby Hunt)

I had to take out the garbage and load dishes into the dishwasher. The main thing I remember is having to mow the lawn and take out the garbage. It took my dad awhile to relinquish the lawn mower. It was a pretty big lawn and pretty steep. I think once he relinquished the lawn, he was pretty excited. I did have some chores, but nothing too strenuous. I think I got an allowance, but I needed more spending money and wanted to be making my own money. I don't know what I spent my money on. Any time I needed money my parents would give it to me so the allowance was silly. Hopefully I'm not too spoiled, but whatever I wanted, they gave me within reason. I don't think I asked for things out of the question—even when the video game thing was big. I just wasn't interested in the big fancy toys. I did have Atari hooked up to the TV in the den. We only had one TV. But I didn't get into the steps beyond Atari like Calicovision and Nintendo when it was taken to a whole new level.

(Cosby Hunt)

I lifeguarded or coached little kids during the summers when I was 15 and older. My jobs were always swim related.

(Adam Vann)

I did a lot of odd jobs for a while like mowing lawns because at the beach people aren't there all the time but they want their lawns to look presentable. So I made business cards and I went around and passed them out. I had five or six lawns I mowed regularly and that's good money for a kid. I made about 150 bucks a week and if you're only spending a quarter on candy canes, if that's your big expenditure you could go buy an ice cream cone and go and buy spend five bucks on games. Five bucks, that was a lot of money back then. Now you go to a bar in D.C. and spend five bucks and it's one Heineken. Back then five bucks was 20 arcade games. That would last me a long time.

(Geoffrey Koontz)

Adam Vann competing in a swimming meet, 1984. (Courtesy Adam Vann.)

TELLING THE STORIES

THE HISTORICAL SOCIETY OF WASHINGTON, D.C.

The Historical Society of Washington, D.C. began telling the stories of Washington, D.C. in 1894—as the Columbia Historical Society. Over the years, the Historical Society has grown up with the city to become a community-based institution that makes history accessible to the public through educational programs, exhibits, research, and publications.

The City Museum's opening in 2003 ushers in a new era for Washington. Welcoming residents and tourists alike, it tells the history of real people and their relationship with the nation's capital. *Growing Up in Washington, D.C.* offers a taste of the complex, yet familiar stories of everyday life in Washington that are presented in the City Museum. From the Native Americans whose artifacts are still found on the shores of the city's rivers, through the Civil War, civil rights, women's rights, tragedy and celebration, tolerance and intolerance, shame and pride, those who passed through Washington and those who stayed have created a hometown that must be known. The City Museum continues the Historical Society's crucial responsibility of preserving the past and the soul of a people who, against a backdrop of events that changed the world, shaped a city unlike any other.

As "Washington's Front Door," the City Museum introduces and orients its visitors to a network of neighborhoods and communities such as Adams Morgan, Shaw, Chinatown, and Anacostia. These neighborhoods, and others, reflect the intersections of rich and changing cultural heritage, artistic expression, economic opportunity, and matchless history. HSW understands that the life and history of Washington cannot be told within the confines of one building. The entire city is itself a museum, with neighborhoods as its galleries and people and buildings as its exhibits. The City Museum's decentralized concept will stimulate and inspire the visitor to explore the grandest aspect of Washington—the city itself.

Washington is a city of crossroads. Traveling along its angled avenues and traffic circles, the intersections in Washington seem more challenging than those in most cities. Intersections define neighborhoods, streets provide boundaries. But the intersections in Washington's history extend beyond the street patterns created by city planners or neighborhood identities into the lives of everyday people.

A special place by any definition, Washington, D.C. has a cultural landscape made up of a unique blend of local, national, and international stories told over time. It is both a place of monumental symbolism and a place of everyday experience. Washington is at the intersection of North and South, rich and poor, black and white, inner city and suburb, local and federal, national and international, native and newcomer. These intersections provide the tension and conflict that make Washington the fascinating city that it is. Intersections are both dividing lines and meeting places; they are destinations that force us to consider where we have been as well as where we are going.

Through the growing up in Washington oral history project, Washingtonians have shared their pathways and experiences through the city. The people who have generously shared their stories of growing up have helped us better understand Washington as a place—like other places—but somehow set apart.

An important part of the District of Columbia's local history is the Central Public Library, the home of Washington's City Museum. Known familiarly as the Carnegie Library and located at Mount Vernon Square, the building is one of Washington's most beautiful and visible symbols of civic identity and community life. Filled with memories of afternoons spent reading in the children's room and checking out books with small, red library cards in the Great Hall, the building holds a special place in the hearts and minds of all Washingtonians as one of the few public spaces that was never segregated. (Courtesy HSW Collections, CHS 09120.)

INDEX